THE SCHOOL IN CONTEMPORARY SOCIETY

THE SCHOOL
IN
CONTEMPORARY
SOCIETY

DAVID A. GOSLIN

Associate Sociologist, Russell Sage Foundation

KEYSTONES OF EDUCATION SERIES

ACADEMIC EDITORS

MERLE L. BORROWMAN, *University of Wisconsin*
ISRAEL SCHEFFLER, *Harvard University*
EDWARD JOSEPH SHOBEN, JR., *Teachers College, Columbia University*

SCOTT, FORESMAN AND COMPANY

Library of Congress Catalog Card No. 65-17731
Copyright © 1965 by Scott, Foresman and Company, Glenview, Illinois 60025
All rights reserved. Printed in the United States of America.
Regional offices of Scott, Foresman and Company are located in Atlanta,
Dallas, Glenview, Palo Alto, and Oakland, N.J.

The study of education is today in a state of ferment. With the expansion of educational horizons in American society, specialists of various sorts—historians, philosophers, psychologists, sociologists, political scientists—are to an ever greater extent joining with professional educators in inquiries into the nature of our educational ideas and institutions. Together, these scholars are enhancing the vitality, authority, and inspiration required of educational concepts in a revolutionary era of social change and scientific discovery.

In some small measure, the Keystones of Education Series is intended to reflect and, hopefully, to advance this educational development. It brings to instructors and students, indeed to all those concerned with education, a unique group of relatively brief but authoritative books, selective in content so as to develop in considerable depth key areas of knowledge. Each book is an original treatment of its special topic. The series may be profitably used in both introductory and advanced courses, for the instructor is free to construct a course with the content, emphasis, and sequence he desires, by selecting a combination of books to serve as text material. Because of the distinguished academic consultants and authorship, instructors can confidently take full advantage of the flexibility of the series without fear of uneven quality, superficiality, or duplication.

The Keystones of Education Series will for the first time make available a variety of superior materials, in convenient and inexpensive format, for the entire pre-service education program at colleges and universities.

The Publishers

TABLE OF CONTENTS

PREFACE

David A. Goslin's book in Scott, Foresman's Education Series is one of the few attempts to grapple directly with the primary tension that affects the American school system. That tension springs from the two strikingly different and often contradictory roles that education is called upon to play in modern society.

On the one hand, the school is clearly an agent of the state—funded by the people and established by them for the straightforward purpose of preserving their culture. As such, the school as an institution is necessarily and inherently *conservative* in its character. With the decline of the family and the neighborhood as vehicles of socialization, this conservative mission of education has been increasingly emphasized.

On the other hand, it has become a commonplace to point out that society has moved into an era of change more sweeping than the world has ever known. Half of all the scientists in human history are alive and working at this very moment. The translation of their efforts into technology has had obvious social consequences that are truly revolutionary. Also, minority groups have at last found both the leadership and the organization that permit their seeking full membership in the community of man. This development in race relations reaches into such diverse realms as the management of cities, employment and commercial practices, and patterns of housing as well as into the schools.

In the face of these new problems, education is hard pressed to contribute meaningfully to their solutions—to play an *innovative* role as well as its traditional conservative one. To help contend with these novel stresses, educators have proposed innovations in services, methods, and curricula. But these proposals cannot be effective without a critical consideration of how the school can best be related to the social order to produce democratic citizens in our tumultuous age.

This thorny problem is what Dr. Goslin's book is about, and it deals with it in a fashion at once quiet and muscular along two fronts. First, Dr. Goslin outlines a conceptual scheme which facilitates a student's perception of the school in relation to a dynamic society, thus allowing a richer understanding of the tensions within education in an orderly relationship to the problems of the American community. Second, he suggests and exemplifies an objective method of attacking these problems, maximizing the use of our developing sciences of man. On both counts, he has made an authentic contribution to our enlightenment.   *Edward Joseph Shoben, Jr.*

During the last half century the field of education in this country has been in a more or less constant state of turmoil. As our society has grown, undergone rapid technological change, and become increasingly involved in world affairs, virtually every aspect of educational policy and practice has been the subject of controversy. Since World War II dramatic shifts in the international balance of power, accompanied by demonstrations of Soviet competence in fields heretofore thought to be the special province of United States technology, have made educational policy a matter of national concern. An increasingly informed public, along with its representatives in the government, has become involved in the movement to reform our educational system. Added to the general concern for the improvement of our schools has been the voice of minority groups who have recognized the importance of education in their fight for equality of opportunity and have taken advantage of the revolution in the schools to express their demands in increasingly militant tones. Professional educators, academicians, politicians, and laymen alike have expressed their views on education with equal force and, more important, assumed authority.

Out of the cauldron of public and professional controversy has come a startling array of opinions, beliefs, facts, and proposals that, in addition to keeping the fires of controversy raging, has led to a number of contradictory developments in American education over the past two decades. Great popular pressure has been generated to improve existing educational facilities and services, but soaring costs in many communities frequently have resulted in the defeat of school bond issues or proposed tax advances. Increased state and federal aid to education has been alternately advocated and rejected. School administrators have been urged to do away with frills in the curriculum and return to an emphasis on basic skills, while at the same time a growing volume of funds has been voted for vocational education, counseling services, programs for the evaluation of pupil aptitudes and interests, and the construction of elaborate physical facilities. Extensive programs have been introduced to facilitate social integration of the society, but recent trends indicate that schools are becoming somewhat more rather than less homogeneous, particularly in our largest cities.

A gradual loosening of family structure has placed the school in the position of having to assume greater responsibility for the total development of the child, while at the same time educational conservatives have called for schools to do away with nonintellective activities. Despite critical shortages of well-trained teachers in almost every school system in the country, relatively more funds have been allocated for new buildings than for higher teacher salaries or for improved teacher training facilities. Although public interest in and support for education has been rising steadily, newspapers and other outlets for public opinion have taken an increasingly critical posture toward the school.

These are only some of the important conflicts and paradoxes that have characterized educational policies and practices. But they serve to indicate both the complexity and diversity of the problems facing those in positions of responsibility for the management of our schools. Educators have had to deal with difficult issues in the past, but never before have they had to make their decisions in quite such a spotlight of public interest. Under such conditions the task of arriving at constructive as well as temperate solutions to pressing problems assumes monumental proportions. School board members and administrators, along with local, state, and national officials who must adjudicate among conflicting demands, are further handicapped by the absence of any explicit set of educational goals and by the lack of any clear-cut body of knowledge about the nature of the teaching-learning process.

The roots of educational unrest lie in the subsoil of a rapidly and dramatically changing society which has begun to make great demands on its educational system and which is likely to continue to create new educational problems at an even faster rate in the foreseeable future. Existing pressures and counter-pressures on educational institutions must be examined in the light of the changes that are taking place in the society and the relationship of the educational process to the ongoing operation and development of the society. In addition to an accelerating rate of technological change that threatens to create a situation in which current techniques and materials are outmoded by the time they are learned and distributed, American society is characterized by a population that is growing in size as well as in mobility, both geographical and, at least in some areas, social. It has also produced a variety of new patterns of social life which are manifested in changing social values and norms and in growing pressures on individuals to develop new ways of adapting to the society. In all of these processes of change and adaptation the school plays a central role in which educational problems reflect the major concerns of the society as a whole.

This book has two primary aims. The first of these is to provide the reader with the beginnings of a conceptual framework that will make it somewhat easier to perceive the school in its orderly relationship to the rapidly changing society in which it is located and thereby to gain some understanding of the social sources of current educational problems. This will involve not only a discussion of the major functions of the school in society, but also an examination of the established ways in which influence is brought to bear on the educational process by the society and vice versa.

In attempting to conceptualize these problems, we have focused on the relation between the various technological, economic, and social changes that are taking place in American society and the school. The first three chapters following this introduction comprise a more or less loosely organized theoretical background for the remainder of the volume, in which an attempt is made to analyze specific aspects of the educational process in the context of the major social changes briefly outlined in Chapter III. In conceptualizing the relationship between the school and the society, the customary sociological distinction is made at the outset between function and structure, although the interdependence of these two aspects of a social system is clearly acknowledged. Chapter I is devoted to a brief examination of the various functions of the school in modern society, including the transmission of culture, socialization, the allocation of individuals to positions in the society, and the role of the educational system in producing new knowledge. Several additional and somewhat less apparent functions are also considered. In Chapter II the characteristics of the social system of the school, both internal and in its relation with the broader society, are considered in an effort to provide a firm basis for the subsequent examination of the way changes in the society are reflected in changing educational policies, practices, and problems.

Chapters IV and V explore the dual roles of the school as an agent of social control and integration as well as in supporting innovation in a changing society. A major theme throughout these two chapters is the conflict inherent in an educational system that is oriented both toward the future and the past, and the implications of this conflict for educational policy. Chapter VI is devoted to the problem of how social changes have affected the school's role in the development and allocation of manpower in the society. Organizational characteristics of the school, including its size, the degree of specialization of roles, personnel problems, communication, and the means by which resources are allocated, are considered in Chapter VII. Changes in the organizational structure of schools are related to the general trend toward bureaucratization within the society, and the implications of these changes for the effective functioning of the school are suggested. In the final chapter the role of education in a society that is rapidly becoming part of an emerging world community is considered, with special emphasis on the new role of the school in helping to prepare world as well as American citizens.

The second major purpose of this volume is to point out the necessity for an objective approach to the solution of educational problems. Educational controversy has been manifested in numerous ways: in speeches by nonacademicians as well as professional educators, in scholarly articles and research reports, in books intended both for the academic community and the general public, and increasingly in the mass media. It has affected everyone connected with the schools, from politicians to parents. While many of those who have spoken out on educational problems have added useful insights to our knowledge about the workings of the educational system, all too often the opinions expressed have served only to cloud already confused issues.

All of the interest in education on the part of such diverse groups is the result of three characteristics of the field of education: its acknowledged importance in the development and future progress of the society, its direct impact on nearly every member of the society, and the lack of any coherent body of knowledge that could form the core of a separate and meaningful academic discipline concerned with educational processes and problems. The first two of these attributes makes the success of the educational enterprise a matter of critical concern to all and in particular to those who hold positions of responsibility for education or for the continued progress and welfare of the society as a whole. Not only are one's life chances influenced in large part by the kind of educational experiences available, but a clear relationship may be discerned between the prospects of the total society for continued prosperity and the vitality of its educational system. Thus the stake in education of each member of the society is very great indeed. Because of the lack of a systematic and verified body of educational principles, those responsible for policy must depend in large part on related disciplines or on information derived from folklore, personal experience, and an unsystematized body of research data of dubious quality for insights into the nature of the educational process.

The effect has been to create a situation in which clear leadership in the search for solutions to educational problems has been lacking. Despite a growing volume of expenditures for educational research, most educators would admit that relatively little progress has thus far been made in providing answers to many of the serious questions that plague the administrator and the teacher. A variety of new educational techniques have been tried out during the past two decades, and innovations in educational hardware have reflected the pace of technological change in the rest of society. But despite ferment and experimentation, no widespread and fundamental changes have been made in teaching methods, curriculum content, or administrative techniques. In basic conceptions and approaches our educational system is much the same today as it was fifty or one hundred years ago.

Nevertheless, the reality of present difficulties in the field of education cannot be denied. As our society continues to undergo rapid technological and social change, it would appear to be inevitable that existing pressures and counter-pressures on our educational system will become greater and greater. All of this raises the fundamental question of what approach or approaches to educational problems afford the greatest likelihood of generating useful solutions and, if innovations are forthcoming, what mechanisms are available for insuring their dissemination and adoption.

One of the great paradoxes of education has been the faith many of those in the field have placed in scientific research to provide answers to all manner of educational problems, only to ignore most of the principles of an organized and systematic approach to the very phenomena they are attempting to understand in their analysis of what is the matter with schools today. For the most part, schools of education have relied on providing their students with a set of guiding principles based on traditional educational philosophy, personal experience, and informal observation, along with a sprinkling of scientific findings from a few related disciplines, most notably psychology. Perhaps because of the fact that a great deal of what has gone on under the guise of educational research has failed to produce anything other than unsystematic and frequently unverified speculations about the nature of the educational process, research findings have not had a very great impact on what is being taught to individuals entering the field or on educational practice in general.

This has led some educators to suggest that our current emphasis on education research is misplaced and that, because of the demonstrated ineffectiveness of most such efforts, we ought to be taking a quite different approach to educational problems (although alternative ways of increasing our store of verified knowledge are not always provided). For example, Robert Ebel has gone so far as to remark that, "to call for additional research has long since ceased to be a novel suggestion. But in view of the record, it may not even qualify as a constructive suggestion."[1] Yet we are still faced with the problem of coming up with intelligent solutions to our pressing educational conflicts and controversies.

A major difficulty with many attempts to do research on the school or to make use of findings from other disciplines to increase our understanding of what goes on in the classroom is the lack of a clear-cut conceptualization of the educational process, especially in in the context of the social structure and functioning of the school and the nature of its response to external influences and pressures. The successful pursuance of the scientific method, whether it be in the social sciences or in nuclear physics, is based as much on a useful conceptualization of the phenomena under study as on the sophistication of the observational techniques utilized. A sterile theory yields sterile research, and a lack of conceptualization results in either productive findings or a basis for theory construction only by chance. The field of education would appear to suffer badly from an over-abundance of observation in proportion to the amount of conceptu-alization available to provide a basis for systematic theory and research. What is needed would seem to be a greater emphasis on conceptualization leading to carefully constructed theory and more *theory-based* research rather than less research. It is hoped that in a modest way the following chapters will provide a small part of the needed organization of thought about educational problems, as well as orient the student toward at least one specific conceptual frame-work within which the school may be viewed.

•

CHAPTER ONE

The Functions of the School

in

Modern Society

•

Before an attempt can be made to assess the impact of changes that are taking place in our society on the school, some attention must be given to the question of what role the school plays vis-à-vis the society and its members. All societies, whether a modern industrialized society like our own or an isolated and primitive tribal society of past or present, are composed of a number of interrelated parts, each of which contributes in some manner to the ongoing character of the society. Every society, for example, must make some provision for collective decision-making if it is to survive for any significant period of time. Similarly, all societies must develop ways of allocating scarce resources, material and nonmaterial, and every society must make some provision for regulating the sexual behavior of its members in order to insure both the continuation of the society over time and the adequate socialization of new members.

The purpose of this chapter is to examine the relationship of that part of the modern society concerned with the maintenance and transmission of culture—the institution of education—to the other parts of the society as a whole. In particular we shall be concerned with what members of the society expect from their schools and how these expectations influence the educational process in the United States.

Each of the different institutions within the society, including the educational system, have important functions[1] in relation to the system as a whole and to its other parts. Thus many of the decisions made by government will have important consequences not only for the society as a whole but also for the functioning of other parts of the system, such as the family or the school. And, conversely, child rearing practices in the family are likely to affect what goes on in the school and, at least in the long run, governmental processes.

The conception of society as a system of interrelated parts is neither novel nor particularly sophisticated, yet it is frequently overlooked in efforts to understand the workings of a particular part of the system. For example, if one wishes to make any real headway in the analysis of the teaching process in American elementary schools, the particular student-teacher relationship must be set in a context that includes some consideration of the various functions performed by education as well as the ways in which other aspects of the social system influence the school. To consider only one of many possible consequences of this interdependence, if certain groups within the society view the elementary school primarily as a place to send children to get them out of the house, then this view of the school's function will almost certainly have an effect on what goes on in the school.

THE TRANSMISSION OF CULTURE

From the standpoint of the society as a whole, and often of groups within the society, the primary function of education is the maintenance of culture. "Man's capacity to learn, to organize learning in symbolic forms, to communicate this learning as knowledge to other members of the species, and to act on the basis of learning or knowledge is the source of all cultural phenomena. . . . Any culture and the civilization based upon that culture must depend upon the ability of the civilization to articulate and transmit its learning as semiautonomous, cognitive systems. These represent the accumulated knowledge in every field of inquiry and comprise the subject matter in all education. This is what we mean when we speak of the school's responsibility in transmitting a cultural heritage."[2]

Culture, of course, includes more than just the "accumulated knowledge in every field of inquiry." It includes the values, beliefs, and norms which have been passed down from generation to generation, albeit with frequent modifications, throughout the history of the society. "Education transmits a common cultural fund to the next generation and in the process helps to bring hordes of young barbarians to adult ways that are continuous with the past."[3]

The transmission and accumulation of culture from generation to generation has been the distinguishing characteristic of man since

the earliest beginnings of human society. The role of formal education in this process has thus been significant throughout only a fraction
of man's history. As Burton Clark points out, "the earliest 'educational systems' were no more than a woman instructing a daughter
or a man and a boy walking, talking, and working together. In the
Stone Age, we may bet, there were no elementary classes in flint
chipping; a boy learned to chip flints by watching adults."[4] As the
store of man's knowledge has grown and the groups in which he lives
have become more complex, the development of specialized facilities
to take over where the family leaves off in this process of cultural
transmission has become necessary. During most of recent history
and extending as far back as the days of the Greek and Roman civi-
lizations, formal education was restricted to a tiny minority of the
society's members, usually the ruling elite or members of religious
orders. The Industrial Revolution, however, in addition to producing
a flood of innovations that caused the reservoir of man's knowledge
and technical skills to burst its heretofore relatively narrow confines,
radically altered the social structure of the society. No longer was
the family the primary unit of production, as was the case in a predominantly agrarian economy. Instead a large number of men (not
to mention women and children) found themselves leaving the home
every day to work in manufacturing plants or offices. This shift in
the basic social structure of the society (which tended to split up
the family unit), together with a growing variety of available occupational positions (each requiring somewhat different skills and
knowledge), made it impossible for new members of the society
to continue to learn by observation of their parents alone. Not only
did the young have more choices as to what skills they might acquire,
than their parents, but no longer did the breadwinner of the family
work where his children could watch him and learn from him.

"In brief, formal schooling became a necessity as the home and
the community became ineffectual, even incompetent, in training the
young for adulthood through informal contact. A new class of cultural agents—the teachers of the commoners—grew up. The changing
nature of knowledge and work brought the children of the common
man into the schoolhouse and gave to the schools a greatly broadened and deepened role in cultural transmission and continuity."[5]

To the extent that current trends in our society continue to
accentuate this separation of occupational and family roles, we may
predict that the function of the school as a primary agent of cultural
transmission will be enhanced. We may not conclude, however, that
the family is no longer important as a socializing agent, or that the
school has taken over all of what used to be the family's functions
in regard to the socialization of the young and the transmission of
culture. Although there appears to be a trend toward admission of

children to schools in this country at earlier ages, the family still serves as virtually the sole agent of socialization during the critical first four or five years of the child's life. It is during this period that the child learns to talk and forms the initial significant social relationships that will greatly influence his adaptation and accommodation in subsequent interpersonal situations. The child also begins to internalize the social values and normative prescriptions and proscriptions that will make it possible for him to function as a member of an orderly society during the remainder of his life.

Nor does the family lose its interest in the child when he reaches school age. In most cases parents, brothers and sisters, and members of the extended family (aunts, uncles, cousins, et cetera) will continue to exert strong socializing influences throughout the period of the child's formal education and, to a lesser extent, thereafter. As we shall see in subsequent discussions, it is likely that many of the special problems with which the school must contend stem from this division of responsibility for socialization of the young. Not only must the school begin with children who have already acquired a set of values (some of which may conflict with values that the school is committed to inculcating), but it must continue to deal with parallel and sometimes competing influences from the family (not to mention the child's peer group) during the time that the child is in its care.

These problems are further complicated by the fact that in this country the school traditionally has been viewed in a service relationship to the family, rather than as a legitimate independent socializing influence. This relationship between the family and the school is perhaps understandable in light of the fact that it is the family that is usually held responsible for faulty socialization and not the school. But this does not make the school's task any easier. Our society has come to expect the school to transmit to the child an enormously complex culture which includes not only a great deal of accumulated knowledge and many complex skills, both intellectual and physical, but an even more sophisticated and complicated set of values and norms which comprise the ideological basis of our cultural heritage.

It is a frequently acknowledged fact that the stability and continuity of our society as presently constituted depends not only on the ability of its citizens to read, write, and complete their income tax forms, but on their belief in and adherence to the political, religious, and social principles on which the institutions of the society are based. Thus the school is expected to teach the child something about such diverse ideals as democracy, the rule of law, free enterprise, and even the desirability of monogamous marriage.[6] And it is also expected to persuade future citizens of the society of the necessity of behaving in accordance with these principles and practices.

Socialization, even within the context of a formal educational system such as the school, involves much more than the learning of skills and the acquisition of information about how the society works or how it should work. Learning that results from more or less formal pedagogical procedures constitutes only a part of the preparation of the child for behaving in accordance with the roles of a participating adult member of the society. Perhaps the most important part of the socialization process involves the unconscious assimilation and internalization of beliefs, values, and patterns of behavior of significant others with whom the individual comes in contact. The preschool child soon begins to emulate aspects of the behavior of his parents, his brothers and sisters, and certain of his peers. As new figures are added to the circle of significant others surrounding the child—his teacher, his classmates, perhaps certain television personalities—the resulting influences on his behavior become increasingly diverse and complex. The possibility of conflict in the emulated behaviors is also increased, and the child must face the task of ranking the people with whom he deals, consciously or unconsciously, in terms of the influence he will permit them to have on his behavior.

Since most children spend a considerable part of their waking hours in school or in school-related activities, it is not surprising that those whom the child encounters in school can have an important influence on his behavior, including the formation of his value system, his attitudes about various social norms, and his behavior in general. It is only through widening his circle of significant others that the individual has an opportunity to prepare himself adequately for the diverse roles which the adult in our society must assume. To function adequately as an adult, the child must learn not only the roles of father or mother but also those of student, teacher, group leader, and, eventually, wife or husband. Boys must learn something about the role of family provider, be he businessman or factory worker; while girls frequently must be able to assume the role of secretary or career woman along with their roles as wife and mother. Although it is obvious that children do not for the most part learn a great deal about some of these roles until they have reached the status of an adult, many of the decisions that a child must make (and in which, although he may receive assistance from his family, his teacher or guidance counselor, or other adults, he is often left on his own) require him to know something about what is expected of individuals occupying various positions in the adult society. In addition, a child begins to acquire more generalized capacities for assuming adult roles at an early age. The school plays a major role, for example, in helping children learn to control their emotions, to deal with as well as assume positions of authority, and to recognize the existence of status hierarchies in social groups.

It is also clear that even if it were deemed desirable to keep children from learning about adult roles, such a course would be impossible without isolating young people from all contact with the adult world. With the rapid development of the mass media, especially television, children are exposed to this world earlier, with greater frequency, and in greater detail than ever before. The influence of the mass media is clearly a fact of modern life that must be considered in any discussion of the processes of socialization and cultural transmission.

A frequently overlooked aspect of the socialization process that has great relevance to any discussion of the functions of the school in modern society concerns the nature of the intellectual process itself. Among other things, socialization involves learning how to solve problems of all sorts. The acquisition of problem-solving techniques is an integral part of the educational process, although this is not always made explicit, perhaps in part because of the current state of our understanding of intellectual processes. It is not completely clear, for example, which of the various ways of going about solving different kinds of problems is of greatest overall usefulness and whether certain techniques are more useful in some situations than in others. Many scholars have advocated an essentially inductive approach to certain kinds of problems, whereas others have maintained that a deductive approach is of greatest usefulness. Learning theorists have not yet fully explored the relative roles of reward and punishment in the learning process, and although during recent years most educators have clung steadfastly to the assumption that optimum learning takes place under conditions of reward, it is not entirely clear that this is the case in all learning situations. Even assuming that some kind of positive reinforcement is most felicitous to learning, it might turn out that rewards intrinsic to the learning situation itself—for example, enjoyment in the activities involved— are all that are needed in certain kinds of learning. The intrusion into the situation of potentially conflicting external rewards from a teacher or parent may serve only to impede the process.

Although new insights into learning and thinking processes are forthcoming all the time, relatively little attention has been given to the problem of how these discoveries relate to what is going on in the school and, more importantly, to what should go on in the school. If one of the most important functions of the school is to teach children how to learn and to solve problems, then it would appear to be reasonable to inquire about what young people are being taught along these lines and whether the techniques they are learning will be of greatest usefulness to them as they assume responsibilities as adult members of the society. Obviously it is important for those individuals who are in positions where they must make decisions affecting the society to be able to adapt effectively to the continually changing demands upon them and to learn how to handle their responsibilities in the most efficacious way. The responsibility of the school in preparing society's members for such positions involves more than the inculcation of technical knowledge along with a smattering of tradition. Of even greater importance is the school's responsibility for teaching the child how to use whatever skills and knowledge he may possess. The educator's responsibility does not permit him to ignore the question of how children are being taught to solve problems and absorb new knowledge. The technique for approaching new information that is acquired by the child in the course of his experiences in school may turn out to be the most important part of the educational process.

SUPPORTING THE DISCOVERY OF NEW KNOWLEDGE

Although the primary function of the school may be the transmission of existing knowledge and tradition, educational institutions have paradoxically also been expected to play an important role in the encouragement and implementation of change. The university has always been a focal point of the search for new knowledge, and a great part of the flood of new ideas and innovations that have produced such rapid change in our society has originated in institutions of higher learning. During the past half century, as the rate of discovery has accelerated, the emphasis on research as a major function of colleges and universities has become of even greater significance. The result has been that the highest academic standing and prestige are increasingly being awarded to those members of the faculty who contribute the most to knowledge and the discovery of new ways of dealing with the physical, psychological, and social world. Much to the distress of many educators and despite frequent claims to the contrary, the teacher in higher education is not accorded prestige and financial rewards commensurate with those received by the researcher. That this trend is having and will continue to have an effect on the quality of the educational process, at all levels, is hard to deny (perhaps, for example, it will improve secondary school teaching by driving dedicated teachers out of the college ranks).

The role of educational institutions in fostering change and innovation is particularly notable at the college and university level, but elementary and secondary schools are expected to play their part in this process as well. Both through the encouragement of creative activities on the part of students and through the inculcation of social values having to do with the desirability of progress based on achievements in the sciences and in other fields of knowledge, the school plays a major role in influencing the rate of change in the society.

Not only does it have a responsibility to prepare children for dealing with the rapidly changing society they will encounter as adults, but if the society is to continue to progress at its current pace, the educational system must continue to produce individuals who will take over the task of developing new knowledge and techniques. As the cultural heritage on which our technology is based expands, the amount of preparation necessary before an individual can make a contribution to our basic store of knowledge grows along with it. The increasing technological complexity of the society has therefore had a profound effect on elementary and secondary education. Even in the primary grades, for example, efforts are being made to revise traditional curriculum content, particularly in mathematics and the sciences, at least in part in order to meet the demands of a society that has accepted change as an ideal to be strived for with all of the resources at its disposal.

ALLOCATING INDIVIDUALS TO POSITIONS IN SOCIETY

Every society must make some provision for deciding which of its members shall occupy the various positions in the society and perform the roles necessary for its continuation and development. Although the number and variety of positions to be filled varies from society to society, it has thus far been true in every society that the available positions have carried with them unequal responsibilities for and demands upon their occupants. Some jobs are more difficult than others, some are more dangerous, and some are more distasteful; some require special training or skills. For this reason and because it is fairly clear that the skills required for some positions are rarer than for others (e.g., the doctor, the judge), the world has not yet seen a society in which the occupants of all positions were accorded equal rewards or status. As a result there is competition among the members of the society (at least within those groups in which competition is permitted) for those positions receiving the greatest rewards and carrying with them the greatest responsibility and prestige. In his utopian *Walden Two*, B. F. Skinner solved this problem by mandating that the occupants of the most distasteful or boring positions would work significantly *fewer* hours but would receive equal rewards from the community—thus making garbage collection a particularly attractive occupation, especially for the artist or musician who values free time more than having an interesting job.[7] Thus far, however, although we have perhaps been moving in these directions, the desirability as well as the possibility of attaining such an ideal is open to question.

Traditionally, most societies have made use of a variety of ascribed or inherited characteristics in allocating individuals to positions or at least in deciding which groups of individuals will have an opportunity to compete for certain classes of positions. Family background, race, religion, order of birth, and sex are examples of ascribed characteristics which have been and frequently still are used as major determiners of the positions an individual may hold in society. However, the rapidly expanding technology of modern society has created a situation in which it has become increasingly important that individuals occupy positions for which they are well suited. As Ralph Linton pointed out in his analysis of status and role in human societies, the better adjusted the members of any society are to their statuses and roles, the more smoothly the society is likely to function.[8] As the requirements for fulfilling various positions become more complex and require not only longer training but greater ability, ascribed characteristics of individuals turn out to be less useful as criteria for allocating positions efficiently than measures of the individual's achievement and ability.

As the school has taken over from the family a greater share of the responsibility for socializing the young, it has also become the focus of many of the child's activities. The performance of the child in school serves therefore as one of the most important early measures of his abilities and energy. With the rise of mass education the school functions as an integral part of the process of status allocation in four ways: (1) by providing a context in which the individual can demonstrate his abilities, (2) by channeling individuals into paths that lead in the direction of different occupations or classes of occupations, (3) by providing the particular skills needed to fulfill the requirements of various positions, and finally (4) by transferring to the individual the differential prestige of the school itself.

In theory, development of public educational facilities in the United States has made it possible for any child to acquire the skills necessary to fulfill virtually any position in the society within the limitations of the individual's own abilities. Although the theory does not always work in practice (we shall examine some of the reasons for this in a subsequent chapter), it is nevertheless true that the school offers most children a unique opportunity to show what they can do. Although we have not as yet reached the point where access to all the different positions in the society is determined by an individual's abilities or even his educational background—ascribed characteristics still play an important part in influencing selection for many positions[9]—the evidence is overwhelming that educational achievement makes a great deal of difference in the kinds of opportunities open to a given individual, regardless of what other attributes he may have.

From the beginning the school operates as the arbiter of the individual's achievement. As the child progresses through the educational system, the decisions that must be made about the kinds of training he may select and the opportunities for advancement open to him are, for the most part, left to the school. The child and his parents may influence these decisions, but in the majority of cases the school plays the major role. It is in this process that the school probably exerts its greatest influence on the allocation of status. The decision as to whether the student will be allowed to take the courses required for college admission, for example, looms as one of the critical choice points in determining the individual's subsequent occupational status.

The skills and knowledge the individual acquires during the course of his education are, of course, important factors in the process of job allocation. But schools are not all equal in the quality of the education they provide or even in the kinds of specific training they offer. Consequently, the individual's long-range occupational opportunities may be determined by the kinds and quality of the educational experiences open to him. We have not yet reached the point where all members of the society have equal access, limited only by their abilities, to the various kinds of training possible. Regional and local differences in resources available for educational facilities, and discrimination in the allocation of what resources there are, severely restrict the opportunities of many members of the society. The situation has been improved in recent years, and the prospect of increased Federal government involvement in education has brightened the picture considerably, both with respect to increasing the total supply of resources available and to ensuring their equitable distribution. As our society becomes technologically more complex, continued progress in providing access to educational facilities will be an important factor in the maintenance of our present rate of growth. Two significant developments in this area, the widespread use of standardized tests in evaluating individuals and the appearance of the junior college, will be discussed in Chapter VI.

Finally, because some schools are better than others, the reputation and prestige of the school is likely to become a factor in subsequent evaluations of the individual, regardless of his actual training or capabilities. Thus the young man who graduates from an Ivy League college may find that there are more job opportunities available to him than to the graduate of a less prestigious college, even though the latter student might be equally qualified. Similarly, the private preparatory school graduate has less trouble getting into many colleges than his public school counterpart (excluding students who attend a few highly prestigious public schools), not only because he may have received better training but in part because of the reputation and prestige of his school. Although there is little data available on this point, the prestige of one's secondary school or college probably makes less difference at present due to the growing demand for well-trained personnel and to the increasing use of objective measures of ability and achievement (e.g., standardized tests) in both college admissions and job allocation. Indeed, one series of studies has indicated[10] that where social class background is taken into account in evaluating the influence of the reputation of one's school or college on subsequent opportunities, the hypothesized relationship disappears. We shall return to a further examination of this problem when we take up the larger question of maximum utilization of manpower in a later chapter.

OTHER FUNCTIONS OF THE SCHOOL

We have briefly considered each of the primary functions of the school in modern society, but like most social institutions, the school has a number of other functions which appear to be tangential to its main role in the society and sometimes tend to conflict with its primary functions. These secondary functions include: (1) the role of the school in providing mothers with relief from the task of taking care of their children during a significant part of the day, which in turn makes possible the addition of large numbers of married women to the labor force, (2) the part played by the school in the courtship process and its consequent influence on mate selection, (3) the use of the school to maintain the cultural identity and therefore the stability of subgroups within the society, and (4) the use of educational institutions to effect social reforms.

THE SCHOOL AS BABY SITTER

In this country compulsory attendance at school fills the gap between the period when the child is almost entirely dependent upon its parents for survival and the age when the individual is deemed able to assume adult responsibilities. During this time not only socialization and intellectual maturation take place but physical maturation as well. In addition to providing a program of activities which fills this gap in a way that is in the long run beneficial to the society, the school also serves as a place to send the children to get them out of the home. Temporary relief from the task of taking care of the children is thereby provided for the mother. The most notable effect of this aspect of the educational process has been to increase the number of roles available to women, including women with children. No longer must a young woman contemplate spending the major part of her life taking care of her children. Instead she may look forward to contributing to the society and the community, as well as to her family, in a number of different ways, while at the same time creating new and meaningful identities for herself in addition to her role as a mother. The effect on the labor force has been to increase the number of females who are holding full or part-time jobs and in general to facilitate the acceptance of women into many occupations formerly closed to them. To the extent that women have become increasingly involved in community affairs, the rise of the club woman and the community service organization run by women volunteers can be attributed in part to this function of the school.

From the point of view of the labor force and the community, the greater utilization of the talents of women is clearly of great benefit. At the same time, overemphasis of the role of the school as a baby-sitting agency may make it more difficult for the school to carry out its major responsibilities in the socialization of new members of the society. As long as responsibility for the outcome of the socialization process is divided between the school and the family, a successful outcome requires the cooperation and mutual support of the family and the school. Where the school is used primarily as a dumping ground for children who would otherwise interfere with activities of adult members of the family, then the mutually supportive relationship between the school and the family is in danger of being eroded. Unless the society were formally to transfer all responsibility for socialization to the school (or some comparable institution) as is being done in Russia, children are likely to respond to the lack of any clearly defined centers of authority by rejecting both the legitimate influence of the school and that of their parents.

Unfortunately, schools have themselves often encouraged this attitude on the part of parents by erecting administrative barriers to cooperation and communication with parents in order to save themselves from the problems created by parental interference in school affairs. The question of finding the proper balance in the relationship between the school and the family is both difficult and of critical importance to the success of the educational enterprise, and we shall return to it frequently during the course of the following discussion.

It should be pointed out that the effect of the school in making possible new roles for women also increases the possibility that members of the family will become involved in role conflict, situations in which they face incompatible demands on their time and energies. This in turn may contribute in some respects to a weakening of the social structure of the family unit. The mother who must choose between preparing dinner for her husband and attending a meeting of the ladies' auxiliary faces role conflict (as does the husband who can't finish his work because he is taking care of the kids). This possibility serves to emphasize our general point that each of the various parts of a social system will influence other parts and that no one aspect may be understood without reference to the rest of the system.

THE SCHOOL'S ROLE IN COURTSHIP

The school also plays an important part in the courtship process by providing a setting in which boys and girls can interact informally and participate in a variety of social activities under the supervision of adults. In this respect the school contributes to the maintenance of the social structure of the community and society by exerting a localizing influence on mate selection. At the college level the institution has a similar conservative effect on social structure because colleges tend to attract students having similar social backgrounds or coming from common geographical areas.

These activities do not necessarily conflict with the school's main functions, and in some respects—namely, the acquisition of social skills—they are an integral part of the socialization process. Students often tend to invest an inordinate proportion of their energies in social interaction, however, and the possibility exists that not only children, but parents as well, will lose sight of the primary goals of the school in the flurry of nonintellectual activities typical of many schools in this country. Where this is the case, the subculture of the student society generates norms and values which pervade the entire community and go a long way toward changing the emphasis of the educational process.

We have pointed out that in addition to its main functions, a social institution may have many consequences for the society, for groups within the society, and for individual members of the society. These consequences need not detract from the institution's primary goals and frequently may complement them. However, when secondary functions assume overriding importance in the eyes of the members of the society, the nature of the institution itself is altered, and this is likely to have wide effects on the social structure and functioning of the society as a whole. To consider the implications of the previous example, if the school were to become first and foremost a place where young members of the society indulged in social activities and found themselves marriage partners and only secondarily an educational institution in the wider sense of the term, the following hypotheses might be entertained concerning the effect of this shift in function on the society: Either the society would have to develop a new institutional form to take over what used to be the primary function of the school (the new form might be called "school," but it would have to be clearly distinguished from the old institution—for example, it might be designated as a "technical school" or "polytechnic institute"), or, if such a new form were not forthcoming, we would predict that the society would be unable to maintain its current rate of technological development.

The reaction of our society following the recent Soviet space achievements demonstrates this kind of relationship between the society and its educational institutions. What happened appears to have been essentially a reassertion of the primary function of the school, the effective transmission of cognitive skills and also of related social values dealing with the obligation of each individual to make the maximum use of his abilities and potentials. This affirmation of the importance of education in this country resulted from the demonstration by the Soviet Union of what an educational institution devoted wholeheartedly to its main function could do and from the related fear that we had gone too far in the other direction. Whether we have as yet achieved or will achieve a properly balanced relationship between the primary and secondary functions of the educational system remains to be seen. There is evidence that we are still moving toward a "tougher" educational system—that is, one oriented primarily toward its main function.

Whatever point of equilibrium is finally reached, it is clear that this kind of conflict and pressure on the educational system is responsible for an additional share of the problems that beset educators in this country. The school will continue to be responsive to the goals set for it by the people it serves, both children and adults. And although educational institutions frequently act to influence the society in which they are located, an understanding of the operation of the system and the decisions made within it depends on an appreciation of the quality of the institution's responsiveness to the society and the character of the particular forces which shape its responses. The more complex these demands on the school are, the more difficult the choices become, and the deeper we must dig in an effort to comprehend them.

With the foregoing discussion in mind, we may return to our consideration of the last two secondary functions of the school. As we have indicated, these are the use of the school to maintain the identity and stability of groups within the society and the use of educational institutions to effect social reforms. Like the other secondary functions of the school, each of these demands may influence the functioning of the school in a variety of different ways or not at all. Whatever their impact on the overall effectiveness of the school, however, they are of great importance in influencing the character of the educational process.

THE SCHOOL AS MAINTAINER OF SUBGROUP TRADITIONS

Since educational institutions have been portrayed primarily and essentially as culture-transmitting agencies, it is understandable that the school will be used to inculcate special cultural traditions and values by many different groups within the society who wish to maintain their subcultural identity. Racial and ethnic groups, religious groups, and entire communities or dominant groups within communities have often made special demands upon the school to transmit a particular set of norms, values, and information. Some groups have established their own educational institutions—for example, parochial or private schools—in order to facilitate the achievement of their goals, while other groups—for example, labor unions, political organizations, and other special-interest groups—have been content to exert influence on existing institutions.

At the same time, public education in the United States has traditionally been organized on a local basis with (at least theoretically) relatively little interference from political or other influences outside the community itself. The result has been the support of local values and traditions by the school and the encouragement of the cultural heterogeneity that has characterized American society throughout our history. As we have pointed out, this is a logical extension of the school's function in the society and is not necessarily disfunctional for the society or for the overall operation of the educational system. However, changes in community structure have led to increasing pressures on many schools to provide a more universalistic cultural tradition. It is this kind of change that has resulted in current conflicts over such practices as Bible reading in the school. As individual communities continue to become less homogeneous, we may predict that public educational institutions will be used less and less frequently to transmit a cultural tradition that is distinct to any particular group within the society.

On the other hand, the transmission of religious beliefs or other aspects of a distinct cultural tradition may be of great importance to particular groups within the society in maintaining their identity. The result, as we have suggested, is frequently the establishment of parochial (used here to refer to an emphasis on a local—or "parish" —viewpoint) or private schools by groups wishing to maintain their cultural solidarity. The Catholic parochial school system provides the most common example of this practice in the United States, although a number of other religious groups provide separate educational facilities for their members.

Nevertheless, some questions have been raised about the effectiveness of the parochial school system in transmitting a distinct set of beliefs. Rossi,[11] after examining a number of studies comparing

Catholics who attended parochial schools with Catholics who attended public schools, concludes that "parochial schools do not appear to be the principal mechanism by which Catholics maintain themselves as a distinct group among the American people."[12] Rossi does find, however, that the parochial school Catholic is more closely identified with his church than is the public school Catholic, and "although he is only slightly more likely to conform to Church requirements concerning ritual obligations, he has a high regard for his religious leaders as guides in public affairs when the welfare of his church is at stake."[13] Rossi points out that, as might be expected, the influence of the parochial school is shown most dramatically in areas where the Church has traditionally taken a strong stand—for example, on support for religious education and on the performance of ritual duties. In other areas of life the evidence indicates that the parochial school Catholic is only marginally differentiated from other Catholics. Rossi concludes that "it would appear that the solidarity of the Catholic group or of the ethnic groups within the Catholic fold maintains itself primarily through other, more informal means."[14]

Regardless of the impact of parochial schooling on the individual Catholic, it is likely that the maintenance of separate educational institutions for the purpose of transmitting a specific cultural tradition has some effect on the rest of the society in general and in particular on the functioning of the public school system. Rossi notes that parents of parochial school children manifest (understandably) a low degree of concern for public schools and for the quality of public school education. In addition to the estrangement of part of the adult population from involvement in the public school system, in many cities the parochial school system is responsible for the withdrawal of a significant portion of the student population as well. Some evidence exists that Catholic children who do not attend parochial schools where they are available tend to be of somewhat lower ability than those who do. Public schools in these areas may find their student bodies composed of only the less able Catholic children along with the other population groups in the neighborhood.

We shall return to these questions in considering the social system of the school in Chapter II. We shall also want to keep in mind these conflicting pressures and expectations concerning the role of the school as we take up the problem of how changes in our society are affecting the educational system and will affect it in the future.

THE SCHOOL'S ROLE IN SOCIAL REFORM

The last function of the school that must be considered concerns the role of education in influencing the course of social reform. Groups and individuals have often attempted to make use of the school as an active agent in effecting desired changes in the social structure or operation of the society. Because of its part in the socialization process and its importance as a major activity in the life of nearly every member of society, the school becomes a prime focus for the social reformer, whether his concern is with the reduction of crime or the improvement of the social position of the Negro. In addition to its function in facilitating the discovery of new knowledge, therefore, the school is frequently expected to play a part in promoting other kinds of desired changes in the society. The pressures on the school which result from this aspect of its relationship to the society may range from requests for the school to provide special services for certain groups of children to demands that school systems do away entirely with racially segregated facilities, even if it means transporting large numbers of children out of (or into) ecologically segregated neighborhoods.

Educational institutions in this country have responded to these expectations and pressures in a great many different ways, although for the most part schools have tended to accept at least a part of the responsibility for social reform that has been thrust upon them. A number of factors including political considerations, budgetary pressures, and, perhaps most important, the attitudes of the local citizenry have influenced the degree to which individual schools or school systems have become involved in reform movements of one sort or another. In recent years organized reform groups such as those representing the interests of minorities have played an increasingly influential role in urging schools to take a more active part in movements designed to alter the social structure of the society.

The line which distinguishes the demand for a new policy aimed at effecting a social reform and the demand for educational reform, per se, is not always easy to draw. It is fairly clear, for example, that both concerns are involved in the problem of school desegregation, and leaving aside political considerations, decisions that must be made by school administrators on this issue are made infinitely more complicated by this fact. The question of how best to improve the quality of Negro education is one which, at least theoretically, is subject to objective discussion based on what we know about learning processes and educational techniques, the subculture of the Negro, and prevailing local conditions. However, the desirability of doing away with racially segregated schools is only partly an educational issue. It is also related to the Negro's desire for equality of occupational and social status and his belief that only through increased contact between members of the two races on an equal footing will significant gains be made in these areas.

As a result of this confusion over the function of the school, it is possible that circumstances will arise (or have already arisen) in which school administrators are going to have to make decisions about policies that in some respects are detrimental to the main function of the educational system but are nevertheless being demanded by groups within the community for reasons based on their desire to achieve essentially noneducational goals. Research now under way indicates that transporting Negro children in large numbers out of ghetto areas to schools in white neighborhoods has, under certain conditions, a detrimental effect on both the receiving and the sending schools, as well as on the achievement and adjustment of the children involved. The best evidence available at present shows that school integration is of definite benefit educationally, at least to the Negro children involved and probably to the white children as well, only as long as the manner in which it is carried out meets certain specific conditions, including the total involvement of the Negro children in the social life and activities of the school. Indiscriminate transportation of Negro children to white schools, or vice versa, without facilitating the assimilation of the children being bussed into the social system of the receiving school (a difficult prerequisite when some children must travel a considerable distance to get to the school and then return to a ghetto peer culture at the end of the day) would appear therefore to be an inadequate solution to the problem.

As has been the case in the past, many variables can be expected to affect the outcome of this kind of decision on the part of school administrators. But if the school is to meet its primary responsibilities to the children of the community, those who are in positions of influence must attempt to distinguish between educational and noneducational uses of the school. The administrator may decide that under certain conditions the function of social reform should take precedence, but in all such decisions the cost to the school and its pupils must be carefully calculated.

•

CHAPTER TWO

The School

As a Social System

•

Sociologists and others have been pointing out for some time that the groups we encounter in society (and the society itself) are nearly always characterized by a more or less definite structure which may be distinguished (but not divorced) from whatever functions they perform. Group members, therefore, may be described not only in terms of their particular characteristics as individuals but also with respect to the characteristics of the position they occupy in the group. Similarly, groups may be studied without any knowledge about the unique persons who belong to them. Most groups of human beings, and in particular those that persist for any significant period of time, may be characterized as being composed of a number of interrelated social positions, each of which bears a more or less clearly (sometimes formally) defined relationship involving rights (status) and obligations (role) vis-à-vis other positions in the group. It is to this fabric of social positions, roles, and statuses that we refer when we talk about the social system of a group.

The occupant of any particular social position, whether it be that of senator, father, wife, teacher, or student, must respond to the legitimate expectations of the occupants of certain other positions (e.g., for the positions mentioned above, constituents, wife, husband, students, or teacher) about how he or she should behave while occupying that position. These expectations define the individual's social role with regard to that particular position. Should the individual fail to behave in accordance with his role, he may be punished by the group or, in extreme cases, lose his position and perhaps his group membership altogether. In addition to expectations and obligations pertaining to the occupant's behavior, most social positions also carry with them the right to demand certain kinds of behavior from individuals who occupy other positions in the system. Thus the student, while expected to behave in accordance with legitimate demands of the teacher, may in turn expect certain kinds of behavior from the teacher. This aspect of a position we will call its social status.[1]

Looked at from this point of view, it is apparent that a large part of an individual's behavior is determined by the characteristics of the various positions he occupies in the groups to which he belongs. This fact also makes it possible for us to learn a lot about how a group works by studying its social structure—the social system with its positions and associated roles and statuses. The purpose of this chapter is to consider the social system of the school in an effort to increase our understanding of the sources and quality of the various expectations that influence the behavior of all those who are connected in one way or another with the school. We shall first consider the social structure of the school itself, without reference to the expectations of individuals (such as parents) who occupy positions outside the school but who may play an important part in shaping the roles and statuses of individuals within the school. In the second part of the chapter the analysis will be extended to include the external influences on the system. In each case we shall be concerned with the effects of characteristics of the social system on the outcome of the educational process—that is, the functions of the school.

CHARACTERISTICS OF THE SYSTEM

THE TEACHER-STUDENT RELATIONSHIP

In most cases the ultimate unit of the educational process is the two-person group made up of the teacher and the student. The specific characteristics of this subsystem may vary widely along a number of dimensions, including physical proximity of the participants, frequency of interaction, the degree to which the student participates in the interaction, and the degree to which the relationship has an emotional component (is "expressive") as opposed to being affectively neutral (is "instrumental" or strictly goal-oriented). The context of the teacher-student system may also vary from a tutorial situation in which no one else is present to the lecture hall containing several hundred students or the totally one-way relationship between the television teacher and individual members of his audience.

Despite these possible variations in system structure, the teacher-student relationship also contains several relatively stable characteristics which should be kept in mind. In the first place the relationship is typically one of status inequality, the teacher legitimately being permitted to make more specific demands on the behavior of the student than vice versa. As the child moves upward through the educational system, he gains in status, and by the time he has reached the level of post-graduate education in a university department or professional school, the apparent status differential that exists between him and his teacher may have been substantially reduced. We would predict that students tend to exert a greater reciprocal influence on the teacher role the farther up the educational ladder they go. It should also be pointed out that because the student-teacher relationship typically involves a disproportionate flow of behavior expectations between the participants, failure on the part of the teacher to live up to the requirements of his role may create problems. This situation is made more complex by the fact that students often are unsure about what constitutes the proper role of the teacher (although there is some informal evidence that many students quickly become rather sophisticated in this regard, particularly by the time they reach high school or college), and the teacher is frequently able to hide his shortcomings behind his institutionalized position of higher status vis-a-vis the student. It is at this point that parents may enter the picture to reinforce the position of the student. The result is often that the school administrator who acts as mediator between parent and teacher finds himself involved in role conflict produced by responsibility to both parents and teacher. More of this later.

Another constant characteristic of the role relationship between student and teacher is that only one of the participants, the student, is expected to change in behavior (as a result of learning) during the course of the relationship. As anyone who has done any teaching will report, a teacher learns a great deal in almost any relationship with a student. But the teacher's role does not *require* him to change in any particular way, whereas demonstrating evidence of learning is an important aspect of the student role.

A third aspect of the relationship which remains relatively stable is related to the preceding point. The teacher role requires that the student be induced to change his behavior in some respect, be it the acquisition of skills in handling numbers or learning how to swim. It is usually the case, however, that the kinds of changes which the teacher is expected to produce in the student and consequently the behaviors that the teacher can *legitimately* demand of the student are more or less clearly defined by the role relationship itself. In sociological terms, the mutual expectations about each other's behavior that are held by the student and the teacher tend to be *specific* rather than *diffuse* (as would be the case in the relationship between a parent and his child). This point requires some qualification in that there are some situations in which the teacher-student relationship may involve somewhat broader and more diffuse expectations—for example, the kindergarten or nursery school teacher may function more like a parent in regard to the generality of her own role (what is expected *of her*) and the kinds of behaviors she may legitimately expect from her pupils than the high school science teacher. Similarly, the teacher in a boarding school may be expected to do more than teach a particular subject; his role may frequently approach that of a parent, and conversely he may demand a wide variety of behaviors from his students.

There can be little doubt that many of the problems that teachers as well as students encounter in the establishment of an integrated and productive role relationship result from a lack of agreement on the amount of specificity in the system of mutual expectations about each other's behavior. Does, for example, the elementary school teacher's role include responsibility for correcting her pupil's manners in addition to teaching him arithmetic? Does it also require her to provide her pupils with love and emotional support in minor or major crisis situations as a parent would under similar conditions? And, conversely, can a child legitimately involve his or her teacher in a family problem by turning to her for support and guidance? These questions for the most part must be answered in the light of a specific situation, but to the extent that our answer to them is affirmative, we tend to make the roles of both the teacher and the student more diffuse, and we consequently increase the possibility that some role conflict will be engendered as a result of overlapping and incompatible demands on the various participants involved.

Turning to the question of the effect of characteristics of the student-teacher relationship on the outcomes of the educational process, it may be hypothesized that where legitimate teacher demands on the student are clearly specified, the amount of time the participants must spend negotiating this point will be reduced, and consequently there will be an increase in the efficiency of the process. Although no systematic data exist in this area, it might further be hypothesized that if, in situations where the role relationship has not been clearly specified, the teacher makes diffuse demands on the student, there will be a greater likelihood that the student will perceive all the teacher's demands as illegitimate. The result, of course, would be a severe disturbance of the teacher-student relationship.

Again, it should be pointed out that we have very little in the way of research findings that would help us to document the preceding argument; at this point we can do no more than speculate, in the hope that this analysis of the system will stimulate others to investigate these problems empirically.

A related dimension of the role relationship between teacher and student concerns the previously mentioned emotional context of the situation. As others[2] have pointed out, the relationship may be "expressive," as in a friendly personal situation, or purely "instrumental," as in a situation designed exclusively to impart knowledge or skills. It is easy to see that an expressive relationship tends also to be one in which the reciprocal role demands will be more diffuse. And the affectively neutral or instrumental relationship will tend to be characterized by specific role demands. There is considerable disagreement among educators at present over what point on the continuum represents the optimum condition for the establishment of a productive teacher-student relationship. As we shall see in our subsequent discussion of the school as a formal organization, pressures which in many situations incline teachers toward the establishment of expressive relationships with their students are generated by the fact that teachers and students are recruited into the organization on the basis of quite different criteria—students have no choice in the matter, whereas teachers are chosen according to achievement—and by the frequent development of powerful student subcultures.

At the same time, there is some evidence that the conventional classroom situation may not foster expressive relationships between teacher and student. One reason for this is that, as we have noted, the teacher-student relationship is defined in terms of status inequality, which puts some limitations on the degree to which a teacher can also be a friend. John and Matilda Riley suggest that one important possibility is that "the type of expressive relationship which makes for effective teaching is not one of equalitarian friendship, but one of admiration of the teacher as a superior and distant figure."[3] In such a relationship the student may permit the teacher to make somewhat more diffuse demands upon him and, at the same time, will use the teacher as a model in the development of his values, tastes, and ideals.

A point on which experimental evidence does exist concerns the degree to which the student plays an active role in the interactional system and the effect of this variable on the efficiency with which the transfer of information is accomplished. As we have pointed out, the student-teacher relationship may vary from a strictly one-way system (as in a television presentation or a large lecture class) to an open interactive system in which each of the participants contributes equally, as in a discussion or seminar. Research findings in the field of attitude change indicate that the recipient is more likely to be influenced by a message when he is given a role as an active participant in the interactive system. In addition, there is some evidence which indicates that it is helpful to the communicator to receive "feedback" from those whom he is trying to influence. These findings support the longstanding educational principle that small classes and discussions are better than large classes with little or no discussion. The same research findings, however, indicate that not all of the possible kinds of recipient involvement work equally well in influencing whether the message will "take" or whether the student will learn what he is supposed to learn. Although educators have been consistent in praising the value of student participation in the student-teacher interactional system, few have extended the analysis to consider variations in the quality of this participation or to consider the possibility that certain kinds of student participation—for example, the irrelevant remarks—might be disrupting to the educational process.

THE SOCIAL SYSTEM OF THE CLASSROOM

Most formal student-teacher relationships are established within a larger social context that inevitably will have important effects on the quality and effectiveness of the formal relationship. Within the school the most important of these larger social systems develops in the classroom. Like any social group the school class can be expected to contain a more or less complex set of social positions having distinct roles and statuses. These positions are generated by the students themselves, although the teacher will probably influence the structure of the social system in many ways—for example, through seating arrangements, the selection of work groups, the recognition of superior achievement on the part of certain students, and the unequal distribution of privileges. Relevant groups and individuals outside the classroom, either in the school as a whole or the community at large, also can be expected to affect what goes on within the classroom in a number of ways to be considered in subsequent sections.

The existence of distinct classroom social systems has been documented by literally hundreds of studies, all of which clearly indicate the importance of an understanding of the characteristics of such systems if one wishes to speculate about the outcome of the educational process. In addition to the empirical evidence available, almost any experienced teacher is able to describe in considerable detail the way in which her classroom is organized, both formally and informally. Students, too, are aware of their own social system and, when asked, can usually provide an accurate description of its structure and functioning. While we know about the social system of the classroom and we recognize that it has an influence on the teaching process, in general we have been slow to analyze the nature of this influence and to take advantage of our knowledge in adapting teaching methods to fit the situation.

For analytical purposes the social structure of the classroom may be viewed as being composed of three different sets of positions. These include (1) the patterns of liking and disliking which create friendship groups, (2) the system of positions specifically related to the accomplishment of the group's primary function—that of learning—and (3) those special positions or sets of positions which provide for group functions not covered by the first two—for example, tension management in the group as a whole. As in any informal social system, all three of these aspects of the classroom social structure are likely to be characterized by more or less constant change, both in regard to occupants of the various positions and with respect to the positions themselves and their interrelations with other positions in the system. Thus the teacher must deal with a constantly shifting social system that is organized on more than one level.

Most of the research which has been done on classroom social structures has been focused on various aspects of friendship patterns, the way pupils in a classroom group distribute their interpersonal preferences. A number of studies have indicated that it is possible to say a good deal more about the liking structure of a classroom group than to substantiate its existence and describe its characteristics. We may distinguish, for example, a number of different dimensions on which the liking patterns of a classroom group may vary and then attempt to link these characteristics with predictions about the academic performance of the group or of individuals occupying the various positions in the system. These dimensions include, among others, the number of distinct subgroups, or cliques, within the system as a whole and the degree to which the system is characterized by a predominantly *central structure,* in which a large number of pupils agree in selecting a small cluster of classmates as friends (thereby neglecting many pupils entirely), as opposed to a *diffuse structure* distinguished by a more equal distribution of liking choices.

One study[4] has indicated that classroom peer groups characterized by a wide range of liking choices tend to have more positive group affect than those having narrowly focused distributions of friendship choices and that a pupil's position in the liking structure of the group is related to whether he makes maximum use of his ability in his school work. The results indicate, for example, that for elementary school pupils who are highly involved in the classroom peer group, significant relationships exist between actual liking status (how much pupils are liked by their classmates) on the one hand and utilization of abilities, attitude toward self, and attitude toward school on the other hand. From the standpoint of the class as a whole, this research would suggest that one technique for increasing pupil motivation is through manipulating the liking structure of the group to make it more diverse, while at the same time attempting to increase the involvement of individual pupils in the peer group as a whole.

Thus far sociologists have barely scratched the surface in the analysis of classroom social structures and their effect on the functioning of the group and on the accomplishments of individual members of the group. As we learn more about the ways in which groups relate to one another and influence their members, new insights into the dynamics of the educational process should be forthcoming. In the interim, teachers must begin to make better use of their awareness of the classroom social structure if they are going to create the most efficient kind of a social environment for learning.

The second aspect of the social system of the classroom involves those positions that are related to the accomplishment of the group's primary function, that of learning. Like all other groups that can in any respect be termed instrumental or task-oriented, most classroom peer groups recognize one or more of their members who occupy positions in the social system that bear a close relationship to the major functions of the group. The child who takes the lead in the various academic activities of the group, whether it be in class discussion or in helping to establish the performance "curve" that will influence the motivation and achievement of the whole group, occupies such a position. The teacher often creates such positions explicitly in the group social system by formally organizing the class and appointing certain children to play particular roles in the resulting organization (for example, work group leader, class secretary, or errand runner). In addition, task related positions (along with the selection of their occupants) may be generated by the normal operation of the group, the teacher contributing to the process by calling on some children more frequently than others or differentially awarding praise for achievements of individual group members, and the group influencing the process because of the varying capabilities and motivations of its members.

A number of studies have indicated that an important determinant of the overall effectiveness of the classroom group will be the degree to which the peer culture supports educational goals as opposed to a variety of other possible group ends, such as having fun. James Coleman, in his recent research on adolescent peer cultures and their effects on the school, provides strong support for the contention that the norms and values shared by the members of the peer group in the school and the classroom have a profound influence on whether teachers can successfully motivate their pupils to perform in accordance with educational goals.[5] In the light of these findings, it is apparent that the relationship between the liking structure of the classroom social system (which will in large part determine—and be determined by—the norms and values of the peer subculture) and the set of task-related positions in the system becomes of critical importance.

The danger in the kind of approach indicated in the previous paragraph is, of course, that although a successful merging of the group liking structure with those positions concerned with the group's main purpose may facilitate the achievement of a large part of the group, it might also serve to accentuate the isolation of particular group members or subgroups that occupy peripheral or deviant positions vis-à-vis the group as a whole. As Riley and Riley point out, "if a proposed innovation were to make use of small discussion groups within the classroom, such groups might be based upon the already existent sociometric networks and friendship clusters. Each such cluster typically has an informal leader, who might be used as a teacher surrogate or a bridge from peer group to teacher. One probable consequence of this would be to perpetuate the alignment of certain groups on the side of conformity, while perhaps failing to motivate the deviant groups and bring them into line with the new program. An alternative would be to manipulate the structure for discussion purposes, so as to merge the rebellious and indifferent individuals with those who are already imbued with academic ambition."[6]

As we shall see when we turn our attention to an analysis of external influences on the school, the problem of manipulating the classroom social system in order to get the most mileage out of the teacher-student relationship is perhaps one of the most difficult that teachers and administrators must face. It is also one of the most important from the standpoint of its impact on the effectiveness of the school.

THE SOCIAL STRUCTURE OF THE SCHOOL

Just as the student-teacher relationship must be viewed within the context of an influential classroom social system, each of the former must also be analyzed in relation to the broader social structure of the school itself. The numerous structural characteristics of a school can be organized under two principle headings: (1) those aspects of the system that are concerned with relations among members of the student body and (2) those that pertain to relations among faculty members and between teachers and administrators.

There are a great many possible ways to organize a group of children for educational purposes. Classes may range in size from a few pupils to a lecture hall full of students, and in ability composition from relative homogeneity to the widest conceivable diversity. Children may remain in the same group throughout the day, or they may move from class to class, encountering in the process a succession of different social systems, each with its own characteristics. Students may be encouraged to do a great deal of their work independently, or the learning process may be structured in such a way that much of a student's time is spent working directly with other students or with the teacher. Whatever the organizational structure decided upon by the school administration, it is likely to have important and interesting consequences for many aspects of the learning process. For example, the range of experiences, both intellectual and social, available to a particular student will be an important factor not only in determining what he may learn but also in influencing his motivation to achieve.

A good example of the way administrative policies influence the overall social structure of the school and in turn the social system of the classroom is the degree to which student assignment to classes is made on the basis of the student's ability and whether the resulting classroom groups tend to be homogeneous or heterogeneous in ability composition. The impact of homogeneous grouping (or the lack of it) on educational outcomes has been the subject of numerous studies by educational psychologists and sociologists. Thus far the results have been anything but clear with respect to the question of whether it is helpful or harmful to group children for instructional purposes according to their abilities. Nevertheless, a great many schools practice homogeneous grouping or "tracking." Whatever the direct effect of grouping on the teaching process, there can be little doubt that the heterogeneity or homogeneity of classroom groups will have an effect on friendship patterns and the composition of resulting subgroups of students within the school as a whole. To take the extreme case, in schools that group children according to their abilities (however measured) we would predict that fewer friendships will occur among children having very much different abilities than in schools where heterogeneous grouping is the rule. It is difficult to predict what effect this in turn might have on the development of student subcultural norms and values or on achievement motivation without a more detailed analysis than can be provided here. It may be noted, however, that because most currently available measures of ability tend to be correlated with the social class background of the student whose abilities are being measured (the reasons for this are subject to considerable debate within social science—some attention will be given to this question in Chapter VI), homogeneous grouping is likely to have the effect of reinforcing social class boundaries within the school and thereby contributing to class crystallization, the degree to which people tend to associate primarily with others in their own social strata.

The preceding question is closely related to the way in which the composition of the community served by the school influences the social structure of the school itself. In simplest terms, the student body may vary from relative homogeneity to great heterogeneity in terms of the social class and racial, ethnic, and religious backgrounds of its members. As the society has changed and grown, neighborhood areas have become more diverse in composition. In addition, there has been a strong trend during the past decade toward the establishment of central schools (particularly secondary schools) serving an area broader than the local neighborhood. The result has been that an increasing number of schools are finding they must deal with the needs of many different groups of students in the context of an increasingly complex social structure. Each of the various groups served by the school brings to it a somewhat different set of values and ideals relating to education. The resulting student culture, although of necessity a compromise between competing forces, is likely to reflect primarily the values of the dominant group in the community. Consequently, the member of the minority group within the school may be faced with a choice between rejecting his own social background and relationships and being left outside the mainstream of school activities. The development of a delinquent subculture based on the rejection of authority among students who are in a minority at school is a common outcome of this kind of situation. This is seen frequently in the attitude of lower-class children toward a predominantly middle-class school system, but it may also occur in a more subtle way in the attitude of members of an upper-class minority toward the rest of the student body and the school in general.

As we have pointed out, administrative policies may tend either to reinforce existing differences between groups of students or to create a common culture by establishing situations in which contact between students of varying abilities and backgrounds is encouraged.

In the same way that the role of the student is influenced by the social structure of the student body, the teacher must also be viewed as a participant in a social system that extends beyond the classroom. This social system arises both as a result of the formal organizational structure of the school and the network of informal relationships established by the teacher during his day-to-day interaction with administrators and other members of the teaching staff.

Every teacher conforms in some degree to the expectations of administrative officers of the school and the school system in which he works concerning teaching methods, subject matter to be covered, matters of discipline, and administrative procedures within the classroom. In this respect the teacher is part of a bureaucratic organization in which he performs specified duties in accordance with the legitimate demands of his superiors. Unlike members of most bureaucratic organizations, teachers traditionally have enjoyed a considerable measure of freedom in their relationship with the administrative hierarchy in regard to the manner in which they fulfill their organizational responsibilities. This has been the result, historically and organizationally, of the autonomy enjoyed by the teacher in the one-room school and the professional status of the teacher in our society. As schools and school systems have grown in size, administrative control over teacher activities has increased significantly, and it is likely to continue increasing in response to the pressures of bureaucratization. As a result, we can predict the likelihood of disagreement concerning the legitimacy of administrative requirements for the teacher role that will have to be resolved if teacher motivation is to be sustained.

Administrative policies also establish criteria for the recruitment and assignment of teachers and for promotion within the system. These in turn will have an impact on such variables as the degree to which the teaching body of the school is hierarchically stratified, the "social distance" between positions in the hierarchy, the amount of mobility that is possible within the system (and consequently the degree to which teachers are likely to perceive opportunities for advancement), and, finally, the bases on which selection for advancement is made (for example, seniority vs. merit). The resulting characteristics of the structure of the teaching and administrative staff will strongly influence the kinds of social pressures and role expectations encountered by teachers located at different points in the system. These expectations will be reflected in the classroom behavior of the teacher; for example, the ambitious young teacher in a system where advancement is based on merit may make quite different demands on his students from those made by an older teacher in a tenure-based system.

Finally, the system of informal social relationships among teachers and administrators within the school has an indirect impact on what goes on in the classroom. A teacher's position in the informal system may have serious consequences for his morale and motivation to do a good job in much the same way that a child's position in the classroom social system is likely to affect his or her performance. Similarly, the informal relationships that the teacher has with the administrative staff will have an important influence on the way he responds to suggestions and directives concerning course content, teaching methods, organizational policies, and the like.

EXTERNAL INFLUENCES ON THE SYSTEM

To this point we have restricted our attention to an analysis of the ways in which various characteristics of the social system of the school contribute to its operation and effectiveness. The internal structure of the system is only part of the story, however. Just as it was necessary to view the teacher-student relationship in the context of its classroom social setting (which, in turn, exists within the broader setting of the social organization of the school), we must continue to widen our analysis to include a number of other relevant social relationships that play an integral part in the educational process. These external influences on the system may be divided up as follows: (1) external influences on the student role, (2) external influences on the teacher role, and (3) external influences on the school.

EXTERNAL INFLUENCES ON THE STUDENT ROLE

In our discussion of the relationship between teacher and student, it was pointed out that each of the participants in this little social system is behaving in accordance with a set of expectations about how someone who occupies one of these positions should behave. In general terms the position of student is established and its role content is determined by the society and the institutional (school) context. In its specific content, the role of student is created in large part by the teacher, and we have already examined some of the theoretical characteristics of this relationship. In addition, the influence of the social system of the classroom has been discussed. However, a number of additional influences on the student role can be distinguished which must be considered if a rounded appraisal of the learning process is to be attained. These include the parts played by the student's family, his peer group, and a variety of other significant reference figures, including mass media personalities.

Because of the importance of the family's part in socializing the child, the influence of parents, siblings, and other members of the immediate family on the behavior of the child in school may be very great. From his parents and his peers the child acquires many of his basic attitudes toward the school and the educational process. In cases where the norms and values of the peer group are opposed to the principles of education, family support of the student role is of critical importance for the establishment of a productive student-teacher relationship.

An important aspect of the family's contribution to the development of the student role is in its influence on the child's feelings about and responses to authority, both inside the home and outside.

As we have pointed out, the student role is almost always characterized by status inequality vis-à-vis the teacher. If the student is
unwilling to accept the legitimacy of the teacher's demands on him,
at least in regard to the subject matter to be taught, no effective
role relationship can be established or maintained. Parents may
create such a situation in either of two ways: by failing to establish
a clear understanding on the part of the child of the necessity and
legitimacy of status inequality *in general,* or by undermining the legitimacy of the teacher's position in specific situations by siding with the
child whenever any disagreement about the teacher's demands arises.
It should be emphasized that although in most cases the particular
requirements of the teacher-student role relationship do *not* require
blind obedience on the part of the student to the authority of the
teacher, it is of critical importance that the *legitimacy* of the
teacher's requirements—especially in regard to specific responsibilities of the teacher—be perceived by the student.

A number of sociologists and social psychologists have observed
that the cultural background of the family group, which in turn is
related to its racial, ethnic, and geographical origins, has a significant impact on child rearing practices and therefore on resulting attitudes about education and authority. It is no secret that some cultural groups—for example, the Jews—place a greater stress on education and the legitimacy of parental and teacher authority than do
others. McClelland has also suggested that an early stress on independence training of children by parents will lead to higher motivation to achieve on the part of children.[7] Talcott Parsons, reporting
on a yet unpublished Harvard study of social mobility patterns among
4,000 Boston high school boys, concludes, "it may be said that the
most important single predispositional factor with which the child
enters the school is his level of *independence.* By this is meant his level
of self-sufficiency relative to guidance by adults, his capacity to take
responsibility and to make his own decisions in coping with new and
varying situations. This, like his sex role, he has as a function of
his experience in the family."[8]

Parents also contribute directly to the educational process by
helping children with their school work and by providing information
and experiences that supplement those the child is having in school.
Riley and Riley point out that the ability of parents to participate
in the teaching process is increasing as the general educational level
of the adult population rises in this country. For obvious reasons it
is clear that, as a group, children from families of higher socioeconomic status in the community will have significant advantages
over children from lower-class families. Data from many studies have
shown that even when children of comparable intelligence are compared, social class background makes a great deal of difference in the

achievement of the child in school. This is no doubt due in part to the fact that parents in wealthier families tend themselves to be better educated and can therefore be of greater assistance both materially and intellectually to their children. The tendency of middle- and upper-class families to instill in their children a greater motivation to achieve in school is also a relevant factor here. Sociologists have also pointed out that children from middle- and upper-class families have an additional advantage in school because most teachers come from middle-class backgrounds and are consequently likely to reward such children for their manner of dress, speech, and conduct apart from their performance in class. Continued research on the influences of parents on children's attitudes about school is clearly needed. In general, however, there can be little doubt that parents play an important part in determining the outcome of the educational process.

As we have seen, the peer culture often plays a major role in influencing the behavior of students. This influence need not be negative with respect to the goals of the school. In many educational settings the subculture of the student group is an important factor in sustaining a high level of motivation and accomplishment on the part of students. More commonly, though, the child's peer culture tends to be oriented away from the educational process in the direction of leisure time activities, recreation, and fun. Where this occurs, the norms and values of the peer group inside and outside the school are at the very least noneducational and, at worst, anti-educational. Coleman has suggested that the family frequently plays a supporting role in the development of a strong peer culture by encouraging the child to arrange for his own recreational activities outside the home. Coleman goes on to point out that we ought either to concentrate our efforts on bringing the child back into the home and thereby reduce the impact of the peer culture on the child or, if this does not appear to be practical as a result of changing characteristics of the family in our society, to recognize the existence of a strong peer culture and attempt to use it to further the ends of the educational process.

The influence of peer groups that exist outside the school has received relatively little systematic attention from social scientists despite the fact that much of a child's time is spent in such groups. Although considerable overlap no doubt exists between a child's classroom social group and his after-school recreational group, up to now administrators have not had an effective way of exerting any direct influence on the latter groups. More attention needs to be given to this problem, however. For example, the increasing number of central schools to which children travel by bus is likely to have a significant impact on the network of social relationships of many who travel some distance to go to school. The resulting decrease in the importance of the neighborhood school suggests that social scientists and educators might profitably consider such things as the conscious structuring of social groups that now arise haphazardly in school buses in an effort to create a supporting peer culture outside the classroom.

In addition to family and peer group influences on the student, a variety of other significant reference figures may affect the child's perception of his role as a student. Of growing importance in this respect are the many different personalities which most children encounter in the mass media—television, radio, newspapers, magazines, comic books, and the like. We are only beginning to understand what makes a child try to emulate a particular television or radio personality. Relatively little systematic research has been done on such broader questions as the impact of television on the school. There can be little doubt, however, that many of the experiences children and adolescents have with the mass media affect their attitudes toward school in general and their role as students in particular. It seems likely, for example, that the extensive television coverage of recent manned space flights with their focus on the men involved served to establish a new set of reference figures for many young people. The increased interest in space science on the part of children all over the country attests to the influence of these developments on the educational process. In a similar manner the mass media can have a detrimental effect on the teacher-student relationship by glorifying rebellious or anti-intellectual behavior on the part of either children or adults or by providing support for peer subcultures that are oriented away from school-centered activities.

In summary, the student role is shaped by many different forces —the teacher's expectations, parents, siblings, the classroom social system, the peer culture, school figures such as the guidance counselor and the principal, and other reference individuals including mass media personalities. And a clear understanding of the behavior of children who are occupying the position of student cannot be obtained until each of the relevant aspects of the surrounding social system are considered. The same is true for the role of teacher, to which we shall now turn.

EXTERNAL INFLUENCES ON THE TEACHER ROLE

As has been suggested, a significant part of the expectations that help to shape the teacher's role come from students, both individually and collectively, and from members of the administrative staff along with other teachers within the school. But there are a number of important external influences that help to determine the teacher's role (and which sometimes are a source of role conflict for the teacher). Chief among the individuals and groups outside the school that are likely to have an impact on teachers are (1) parents of students, (2) professional reference groups, including the faculty at the college or university where the teacher was trained, and (3) the teacher's family and friends outside the school.

Because of the previously mentioned relationship of status inequality between teacher and student, the teacher seldom encounters open challenges to his authority from students. On the other hand, parents often try to exert an influence on teachers, particularly where questions are raised about the legitimacy of teacher demands on their children.

School situations vary considerably in regard to the amount of contact between parents and teachers. Lack of contact may result from a reluctance on the part of the school to become involved in possible parental pressures, to physical barriers such as the distance parents must travel to reach the school, or to simple indifference. But even where there is relatively little opportunity for teachers to meet with parents on a face-to-face basis, the influence of parents on teacher behavior may be very great both in general terms and in specific cases. Teachers are aware that parents will be judging the results of their efforts and that students are likely to report to their parents on the characteristics of their teachers. Teachers also must communicate periodically with parents concerning their son's or daughter's performance in school. Despite the presumed professional status of the teacher, his relationship to parents is frequently defined in service terms, because parents retain the ultimate responsibility for socialization of the child. In its most basic terms, this general problem is reduced to the question, "to whom does the child belong?" The marginality of the teacher's professional status is clearly seen in the contrast between the answers that would be given to this question in situations where a doctor's or lawyer's advice is required and those that would be given in analyzing the parent's relationship with the school. The degree to which parents are likely to perceive the teacher as being responsible to them for educating their child and therefore actively attempt to influence the teaching process will be related to such variables as the relative social class backgrounds of the teacher and the family, the extent to which the community in general takes an active interest in the school, and the degree to which the subject matter is of a highly specialized nature.

As mediator between teacher and parents, the administrative staff of the school plays an important part in determining the amount and character of the influence that parents may bring to bear on the teacher. The principal may substantially reduce the effect of parental pressure by making it difficult for parents to see teachers, by handling questions of discipline himself, and by making it a policy to support teachers wholeheartedly where questions concerning particular student-teacher relationships arise. On the other hand, the principal may let teachers handle the majority of disciplinary problems themselves and encourage parents to go to the teacher whenever problems are encountered. While the latter course of action is likely to lead to more parental involvement in school activities (or at least in one kind of school activity), it also increases substantially the possibility that the teacher will find himself in situations characterized by role conflict where he is unable to respond adequately to all of the demands made upon him. In such situations, teaching loses not only some of the characteristics of a profession but also, perhaps, some of its attractiveness as a way of earning a living. What is being suggested here is *not* that teachers should be insulated from parental contact and influence but that administrators must be cognizant of the fact that some control needs to be maintained over what demands parents may legitimately make of teachers if role conflict is to be avoided and the integrity, autonomy, and professional status of the teacher is to be maintained.

In attempting to understand the behavior of the teacher, it is of critical importance that it be recognized as resulting from a highly complex and sometimes conflicting set of expectations that stem not only from significant others with whom the teacher interacts while carrying out her job—students, administrators, other teachers, and parents—but also from individuals and groups that the teacher comes in contact with or relates himself to outside of school. The teacher's spouse, children, and parents all are likely to exert an influence on his behavior by making known their feelings about how an occupant of the position of teacher ought to behave. Similarly, during the course of the teacher's own educational experiences, he will have absorbed many different impressions of what constitutes proper behavior for a teacher, and he is likely to compare his own performance in this position with that of one or more of his former teachers who thereby serve as reference figures.

EXTERNAL INFLUENCES ON THE SCHOOL

Schools, like teachers and students, do not exist in a social vacuum. They are usually part of an administrative network made up of all the schools in a single district (a number which may range from one or two to several hundred) under the supervision of a superintendent of schools and the local board of education. They also function within a neighborhood social system (in which they may play a more or less active part), a community or local political unit, a state educational authority, a geographical region having definite social characteristics distinct from those of other regions of the country, and finally, a nation having a common federal government and a cultural heritage that provides the school with much of what is to be taught to its students. With respect to these variables, no two schools can be said to be completely alike, since within school systems neighborhoods vary, and though we may find comparable neighborhoods in different parts of the country, regional and community differences exert overriding influences in each particular case.

The importance of an appreciation of the ways in which external factors influence what goes on in particular schools cannot be overestimated. Without taking into account demographic characteristics of neighborhood areas, local political considerations, or unique regional cultural traditions, the social scientist or the educator is severely handicapped in attempting to understand the reactions of teachers, students, and administrators to the various problems they encounter in the course of their daily routine. In order to lay the groundwork for subsequent analyses of the impact of social change on various aspects of the educational process, we shall try to describe briefly a few of these external influences on the school. At this stage in the discussion, our aim is primarily to sensitize the student to the fact that the social setting of the school may be a significant factor in determining what happens in the classroom and to at least enumerate some of the social variables that are likely to intervene in the influence process.

In a great many schools a significant portion of school policy, in regard to both administrative matters and curriculum content, is determined by officials at the system level—the superintendent of schools and members of his staff. The degree to which school personnel participate in system-wide decisions about matters relating to the everyday activities of individual schools varies greatly and is likely to be based on such diverse factors as the size of the school district and the personal relationship between the principal and superintendent. During recent years there has been a tendency (despite some evidence of a countertrend in huge systems like New York) for school districts to become somewhat more centralized and for more system-wide functions—for example, standardized testing programs—to be taken on by the office of the superintendent. Aside from the advantages of increased efficiency and economy, it seems likely that one of the reasons for this development lies in the tendency of the public to focus its attention on the tax-collecting agency as the responsible body to which complaints, recommendations, and opinions about what is or should be happening in the schools are directed. As school boards have asked their communities to support school bond proposals and tax increases aimed at improving the schools, citizens have responded by asking the superintendent of schools through the board of education to justify these requests. Faced with these pressures, it is not surprising that superintendents have felt it necessary to exert increased control over educational policy in the schools. This control has been extended into such critical areas as teacher selection, administrative organization of the school (for example, homogeneous grouping), textbook selection, and evaluation of the outcomes of the educational process (for example, through standardized testing). All of these are in addition to areas of school construction and maintenance, for which the superintendent has traditionally been responsible.

One of the most jealously guarded characteristics of education in the United States has been the freedom of each community to organize and run its own schools. As elected representatives of the local citizenry, the lay Board of Education has traditionally played an important role in governing the school system in most communities in this country. As has been indicated, the superintendent of schools is typically appointed by and is responsible to the Board of Education, and it is through the superintendent that the influence of the board is exerted on educational policy in the community. The relationship between the board and the superintendent of schools marks one of the most important points of contact between the public and its schools. As a result, problems often arise at this point that not only affect the functioning of the schools but create role conflict for the superintendent. Pressures may be brought to bear on the superintendent to cut costs radically; to make use of the school system to effect social reforms—for example, racial or religious integration—or to hire teachers of a particular type. Because the superintendent has a responsibility both to the board of education and to the school system, he is frequently faced with situations where he must resolve incompatible demands—for example, from the teachers for higher salaries and from the board to trim the budget—in such a way as to appease the board and achieve the main goals for which the schools were established. As some social scientists have pointed out,[9] this is not always accomplished with ease or to the satisfaction of all of the parties involved, particularly as schools develop more complicated bureaucratic structures and education in general becomes technically more difficult for the public to understand.

It is this interplay of influence between the school system and the public that forms the backdrop for the setting of educational policy in the schools and eventually for the establishment of effective relationships between teachers and students. The political, economic, and social makeup of the community will have a lot to do with the kinds of pressures that the superintendent will encounter and, ultimately, with the way the schools are run. In addition, from the standpoint of particular schools within the community, the degree to which interests of neighborhood groups served by the school are represented by the board of education may determine in part how much voice individual parents have over the kind of education their children are getting. It may not be enough for a parent to speak to the school principal in situations where the principal is acting on the basis of a system-wide policy, and if the group to which the parent belongs is not represented at the level of the board of education, there may be little recourse.

Some of the economic and social variables that are likely to be reflected in local pressures on the school system and individual schools within it include the following:

(1) The wealth of the community and the availability of this wealth for educational purposes. This in turn will be determined by such factors as the amount of industry (which usually provides an important source of tax revenue) in the community and the degree to which citizens are willing to spend their money on schools. While middle- and upper-class suburban residential communities have been most willing to finance their schools adequately, even without the benefit of taxable industry within the community, many such areas are beginning to feel the squeeze as the costs of education (along with other local governmental costs) continue to increase. At the same time, the tax problems of large cities that must provide many expensive services for a sizable nonresident (and therefore nontax-paying) population are also reflected in severe shortages of funds for educational purposes.

(2) Related to the factor of wealth is the social class, racial, and ethnic makeup of the population in the community. As we have pointed out, different groups within the population hold different views of the educational process. Some groups, in particular middle-class and upper-middle-class groups, tend to be more willing to support education and to take an active interest in the formation of educational policy, while other segments of the population may perceive the schools primarily as means to the end of maintaining a subcultural identity or of effecting social reform. Each of these various points of view will be reflected in the pressures placed on the school system, particularly if the group holding the dissident view happens to be the dominant group in the community (or can obtain the sympathy of the dominant groups).

(3) The age structure of the population is also likely to have an important effect on the schools. Communities having a disproportionate number of families with children as opposed to single men and women, childless couples, and old people are likely to be characterized by greater interest in and support for the educational system. This can be seen clearly in the case of suburban residential communities.

(4) A fourth factor is the rate of change in the community, in terms of both population turnover and technological change. Communities characterized by a highly transient population, even though predominantly one with children, may take less of an interest in their schools than more stable communities. Such a community may also find it more difficult to hire and hold good teachers and administrators, although this will depend on other factors in turn, such as the availability of a university or teacher-training center nearby.

(5) Finally, regional as well as local differences of opinion about what constitutes the proper function and organizational structure of the school will be reflected in particular school policies. Southern beliefs about the desirability of racial segregation, extreme right-wing political beliefs about what should and should not be taught in history and civics courses, and the feelings of many citizens groups relating to questions of whether children should be allowed to read controversial books are all examples of beliefs that help to form the climate of public opinion within which the board of education, the superintendent of schools, and individual school administrators must work.

The educational system is also subject to attempted influence by many organized associations of laymen. As Robin Williams puts it, "the number of these organizations is uncalculated but extremely large and includes all major types of organizational interests in our society. The larger and more effective include business, labor, patriotic, religious, benevolent, youth, citizen-training, military, peace, fraternal, and political organizations. There are pro-minority and anti-minority groupings, associations of reactionary, conservative, liberal, and radical inclination. Each is devoted to its own version of the American Way of Life, and few leave the schools to train youth without outside guidance."[10]

Although ultimate control over educational policies still remains almost entirely in the hands of the local board of education, both the state and federal governments have had an increasingly important role in local education during the past two decades. The state share of total appropriations for public schools increased from 16.5 per cent in 1919-1920 to 39.1 per cent in 1959-1960.[11] State departments of education have begun to take an active part in setting educational standards for local schools and in enforcing state regulations concerning the management and operation of schools. The development of standardized achievement tests in many fields of study has prompted the establishment of state-wide testing programs in several states, including most recently California, which now requires all schools in the state to test children in grades five, eight, and eleven with tests chosen from an approved list of commercially published standardized instruments, in three different fields: reading, arithmetic, and language usage (as well as basic intelligence). Although typically no minimum performance levels are set by the states having such programs, there is little doubt that schools and students feel the impact of such testing. The New York State Board of Regents Examination Program has been in effect for more than half a century. Although recently the Regents tests have been criticized for allegedly deleterious effects on teaching methods and curriculum innovation, most educators have been willing to concede that they have been instrumental in raising educational standards generally.

State legislatures have for some time set requirements for teacher certification in their respective states[12] and have passed laws covering such matters as the number of days in the school year. In the wake of recent Supreme Court decisions relating to the schools, a few states have begun to take an interest in such controversial local issues as integration and the observance of religious rituals in schools. As a result of these actions the potential influence of state education departments on school systems has been increased. Similarly, the federal government, primarily through court decisions and new programs of aid to schools, has become involved in the complex system of external influences on local schools. The federal government spent over two and a half billion dollars on education in 1959-1960, and this figure has been substantially increased since then. Thus far, no integrated federal program has been forthcoming in the field of education despite the sizable investments that have been made. At present there are at least two hundred separate programs in operation, aimed at various levels of the educational system.

Up to now, federal aid to education has had little direct or detailed influence on schools other than general support through such activities as the free lunch program or encouragement of particular areas such as vocational education and the development of special curricula for handicapped children. The strong fear of centralized control over education has been partly responsible for this scattered and uncoordinated federal effort. Every indication supports the view, however, that we shall see more and more government intervention in the field of education. A major stimulus to such intervention has been the significant role played by the federal courts in ruling on issues of major importance directly involving the schools. What this means is that the local board of education, superintendents of schools, principals, and even teachers can no longer respond only to the pressures and demands of local interest groups. Instead there is developing a national concern with educational policy that is and will continue to be reflected in legislation relating to the school, including at least indirectly, what is to be taught there.

•

CHAPTER THREE

The Impact of Social

and

Technological Change

•

One of the relatively stable characteristics of American society has been its rapid rate of change. In this country high value has always been placed on conditions that foster innovation and change. Though frequently resisted by those members of any society who stand to lose as a result of change, the innovator has received more encouragement here than in almost any other place at any other time in history. This has been particularly true in recent years, as an expanding store of information and techniques has been combined with a growing population and a plentiful supply of resources, both material and intellectual, in the highly competitive context provided by a free enterprise system. As Burton Clark has pointed out, "modern man is clearly in a second scientific revolution. The first revolution centered on the steam engine and the spinning machine and put machines in the place of muscle. The second scientific revolution (occurring in the last forty years and especially since 1945) centers on atomic energy, automation, computers, and chemical materials. It greatly magnifies technically produced energy, changes processing methods, alters the materials on which men and machines work, and often substitutes machines for human thought and control. Although we have been sliding into a technological age on the basis of accumulated techniques produced by the first scientific revolution, we are now in for technology with a vengeance. Through its ramifying effects—technology alters nearly all institutions."[1]

Technological innovation is, of course, only one dimension of change in society. A significant characteristic of human societies, however, is the extent to which culture and social structure are interrelated. Thus a new invention is likely to lead to both normative and structural changes in the society and vice versa. Change also occurs at all levels and in all parts of the society, although not necessarily at the same pace in each area. One would be hard put to find a member of our society who has not felt the impact of social and cultural change of one sort or another many times during his lifetime. The same effect, multiplied by the experiences of their members and often made more stressful by the existence of established procedures and norms, is felt by organizations and groups. While it may not be necessary to provide detailed documentation for the statement that our society is currently undergoing rapid social and cultural change, our concern with the impact of change on the educational process requires that some consideration be given to a classification of the major areas of change in America at the present time. In addition, we shall want to consider briefly the question of what generalizations may be made about social change with respect to its general nature, in an effort to gain a better understanding of the forces that produce it.

In *Social Change,* Wilbert Moore summarizes the peculiar features of contemporary change as follows:

1. For any given society or culture rapid change occurs frequently or "constantly."
2. Changes are neither temporally nor spatially isolated—that is changes occur in sequential chains rather than as "temporary" crises followed by quiet periods of reconstruction, and the consequences tend to reverberate through entire regions or virtually the entire world.
3. Thus, since contemporary change is probable "everywhere," and its consequences may be significant "everywhere," it has a dual basis.
4. The proportion of contemporary change that is either planned or issues from the secondary consequences of deliberate innovations is much higher than in former times.
5. Accordingly, the range of material technology and social strategies is expanding rapidly and its net effect is additive or cumulative despite the relatively rapid obsolescence of some procedures.
6. The normal occurrence of change affects a wider range of

individual experience and functional aspects of societies in the modern world—not because such societies are in all respects more "integrated" but because virtually no feature of life is exempt from the expectation or normality of change.[2]

Thus Moore emphasizes both the normality and interdependence of change in modern societies, while at the same time pointing out the hazards of social life in an age when procedures that are appropriate for a task today are obsolete tomorrow. In the light of these characteristics of our society, many of the pressures and counter-pressures on the school become more understandable. Because of their dual functions as agents of both innovation and social control, schools occupy a uniquely central position in a developing society. Educational institutions have had forced upon them the task of preserving that delicate balance between stagnation and chaotic change. The school is expected to train members of the society to think creatively and to provide them with the skills necessary to continue to create change, while at the same time inculcating a cultural heritage based upon adherence to existing norms and traditions.

In the remainder of this chapter we shall concentrate primarily on describing some of the most important areas of change in American society, while indicating a few of the implications for education in each case. The following analysis, along with the material presented in the preceding chapters, provides the theoretical background for the more detailed discussions of critical educational problems that constitute the remainder of this volume.

TECHNOLOGICAL CHANGE

The technology of a society is that aspect of its culture that is primarily concerned with the capacity of members of the society to adapt to their environment, both physical and social. Thus every society possesses a technology, although the degree to which control over the environment is effectively exerted and the complexity of modes of adaptation vary widely from society to society. In societies having a highly developed technology, such as our own, basic adaptation to the physical environment is virtually complete, and an increasing proportion of the society's technological energies is devoted to the solution of problems generated by the *social* environment (for example, the use of computers for analyzing data about organizations and individuals) and to *changing* or *expanding* the physical environment as opposed to adapting to it (for example, controlling weather and exploring space).

As we have already indicated, the rate of technological innovation is directly related to the size and sophistication of the existing cultural base. As our society has become more advanced, the *rate* at which innovations have been forthcoming has increased. We are now faced with the prospect of dealing not only with a technology that is changing but with one that is changing at an accelerating pace.[3] It is of interest to speculate about whether the current acceleration of technical development will continue until the society eventually shakes itself apart as a result of its inability to adapt to the changes it has produced, or whether the rate of change will eventually diminish as we exhaust the potential of our scientific skills to produce new knowledge.

It should be made explicit that technology involves more than hardware and that technological development goes beyond the invention of a new kind of airplane, rocket, or hairdryer. More significant than the new products that result from a changing technology are the new techniques, procedures, and skills that are responsible for their development and production. It is new ways of doing things that make possible both current advances in our material well-being and the innovations that continue to extend our technological horizons to provide us with visions of what might be.

As the society changes technologically, it is apparent that the educational system must keep pace with it. Not only must schools turn out individuals who are capable of keeping the machines on which the society depends running, but even more importantly they must also provide the remainder of the population with the knowledge, skills, and sophistication necessary to adapt successfully to the multitude of changes occurring around them and to solve whatever new problems are generated by current technological innovations. This is necessary if we are merely to keep up with ourselves. If continued development and change are deemed desirable, schools must assume the added responsibility of preparing certain members of the society to take an active part in the change process.

The primary effect of all this on the school is to make mandatory continual changes in what is taught, even at fairly basic instructional levels. As computers have increased in complexity and usefulness, for example, changes in the elementary mathematics curriculum have become necessary in order that new members of the society may be able to make more efficient use of the tools available to them. As our knowledge of the principles of physics, chemistry, and biology expands, in both theoretical and practical terms, the content of secondary school courses in these and other subjects must be altered to accommodate our new insights. Similarly, but at a different level, as new and increasingly specialized techniques and knowledge become necessary in many different blue collar occupations, from the mechanical trades to agriculture, vocational training in these areas not only becomes more important but requires continual overhaul.

All of this makes it increasingly important for teachers to change their orientation towards their subject matter—to approach it as a changing body of knowledge rather than as a fixed and immutable set of facts and principles. Up to now the former attitude toward knowledge has been characteristic of the university scholar but only rarely of the primary or secondary school teacher. From the standpoint of the latter group of teachers, this represents a potentially revolutionary alteration in the requirements of their jobs. The elementary or secondary teacher has not been required to "keep up with the literature" in the same way that the university or college teacher is expected to keep abreast of new developments in his field. Consequently, it has not been the practice to make allowances for this requirement of the job when establishing teaching loads for such teachers. The impact of requiring increased scholarship of elementary and secondary school teachers on such things as school budgets, salary scales, the availability of library facilities and the recruitment and training of new teachers is not difficult to imagine. It should be pointed out that some steps in this direction have been taken already —for example, in the establishment of summer re-training centers (and the provision of fellowships for teachers to attend them) and in the use of "master teachers" who are given time off to prepare for the presentation of specialized subjects. Although these have been needed and useful innovations, we have thus far barely scratched the surface in attempting to solve the broader problem of how to keep already overworked teachers abreast of new developments in their fields and in the society generally.

Related to the above-mentioned needs for constant curriculum change is the fact that the increased complexity of our technology tends to make necessary more specialized training at an earlier age if we are to avoid stretching out the educational process interminably. This has implications for the process of manpower allocation and the identification of talent (which will be discussed in Chapter VI) as well as for changing curriculum requirements at the primary and secondary levels.

Finally, the technology of the education itself is changing in response to changes in what has to be taught, the availability of new techniques of communication and related innovations, and as a consequence of increased knowledge about the nature of the learning process. We shall return to these points in Chapter V and Chapter VII.

BUREAUCRATIZATION AND SPECIALIZATION

Associated with the increasing technological complexity of the society has been the growth of large bureaucratic organizations characterized by a hierarchy of formally defined positions each having a well-defined role and status as well as a specialized function in the organization. Bureaucratization and the concomitant increase in the size of organizations throughout the society (including education) has resulted from two related factors: the search for greater efficiency in the accomplishment of fairly complex tasks (such as the production of automobiles or electronic computers) and the growing degree of technical proficiency required at every stage in the process. The effect has been to create larger and larger organizations based on a finer division of labor. Although much maligned as a result of their allegedly dehumanizing characteristiqs, it is not likely that there will be any significant reduction in the prevalence of bureaucratic organizations during the decades to come. And there is every indication that existing organizations, from governmental agencies to private corporations, will continue to grow in size and complexity.

The effect of bureaucratization on the school has been threefold. From the standpoint of what the student is expected to learn and the opportunities open to him, there has been a tendency for the school to transmit society's demands for increasingly specialized skills to students in the form of more specialized courses, the necessity for earlier decisions about vocational as opposed to academic preparation, greater emphasis on aptitude as well as vocational interest tests in an effort to classify children according to their interests and abilities at an earlier age, and more formalized requirements for promotion and, eventually, graduation or certification. At the same time the teaching process itself, along with the internal structure of school, has become more highly organized. Homogeneous grouping, tracking, and the establishment of special groups for children with special problems or abilities have become standard educational practice in a great many schools. More efficient uses have been made of teacher time and effort by such practices as team teaching, the use of master teachers, television lectures, and the introduction of specialists in areas like reading and foreign language instruction. These innovations have been made both possible and necessary by the increasing size of schools and the changing public conception of the school from an informal gathering place for children of all ages and abilities presided over by the stern but kindly spinster lady to an efficiently functioning organization staffed by well-trained professionals.

Societal tendencies toward specialization of function, bureaucratization, and increasing size also have been reflected in the growth of much more complex administrative hierarchies in many school systems. For the past several decades the number of school districts in existence has been reduced at an accelerated rate as a result of reorganization and consolidation of small units. According to the latest U.S. Office of Education figures, the number of school districts fell from 40,500 in 1959–1960 to 31,700 in the fall of 1963 (consisting of 27,800 operating districts and 3,900 nonoperating districts),[4] a decrease of 21.7 per cent in a four-year period. As school districts have grown in size, problems of coordination and administration have increased at an even faster rate. Combined school districts have made possible greater efficiencies in the teaching process, as we have indicated, but they have also produced some new problems for the administrator—for example, the often exceedingly complex task of getting children to school in situations where bus transportation must be provided. Running a school system has become a big business in many places. The resulting administrative hierarchy often closely resembles the major corporation or government agency. In New York City the annual budget of the school system which must assume centralized responsibility for the city's more than eight hundred public elementary and secondary schools is nearly a billion dollars. Some of the ramifications and implications of increasing organizational complexity will be examined in Chapter VII, but it should be emphasized here that administrative problems—the construction and maintenance of adequate buildings, the provision of needed supplies from soap to chalk, or the operation of a cafeteria capable of serving nourishing lunches to children who are unable to go home for lunch—cannot be separated entirely from "pure" educational concerns like the optimum size of classes or the content of mathematics courses. Financial resources must be allocated among various competing uses, and what is spent for heating the school in winter (or airconditioning it in warmer months) or providing school buses for pupils is not longer available for teacher's salaries or text books. If children are forced to travel exceptionally great distances to get to school, either because of the size of the school district or the complexity of the bussing problem, their academic performance may be impaired. The physical facilities of the school will have much to do with the kinds of educational experiences—from dramatics to music to science experiments—that can be provided for children. Thus organizational and administrative problems, mundane as they may seem, are of critical importance to a consideration of the school and social change.

DEMOGRAPHIC CHANGES

During the last half century a number of important changes have taken place in the size, distribution, and composition of the population in the United States. Current trends indicate that the population structure will continue to change during the decades to come. Since the educational system must be responsive to changing populations, each of the major shifts in population is likely to have ramifications for educational policy and problems at various levels. Perhaps the most noticeable change has been the overall growth of the population, which now totals approximately 190 million persons. During the last decade the population of the United States has been growing at the rate of about three million a year with a cumulative increase of about 19 per cent during the ten-year period, nearly all of which was due to an excess of births over deaths as opposed to net immigration. This is a much faster rate of increase than in the period prior to 1940, which may be attributed to a trend toward slightly increased family size expectations and the postponement of depression and World War II births.[5] As a consequence of the higher birth rate, the median age of the population has been lowered from 30 in 1950 to 29 in 1960, and the school age population has increased rapidly, particularly in contrast to the size of the depression years cohort which is now age 24–32.

The impact of this increase on the educational system has been very great, and even in the most prosperous areas school districts have been hard pressed to keep up with the influx of new pupils. The situation has been further complicated by the fact that some areas, particularly suburban communities, have had to handle a disproportionate share of the increase. According to Eleanor Bernert and Charles Nam, "approximately two-thirds of the national population increase in the past ten years is found in metropolitan areas and almost all of this in the suburbs."[6] An Office of Education survey indicated that in the three-year period between 1953 and 1956 the rate of increase in public school enrollments in suburban areas was more than twice that for related central cities.[7] Because of the particularly acute educational problems faced by these areas, as well as those of the central city, the following section will be devoted to a discussion of the processes of urbanization and suburbanization.

During the last thirty years the racial composition of the total population has remained relatively unchanged (about 10 per cent of the population is nonwhite),[8] but selective migrations have produced marked changes in the makeup of certain areas, most notably urban regions in the Northeast and Midwest. Major labor markets in these areas, and to a lesser extent in some Western cities, have attracted a large number of Negro migrants from the South who have typically been forced to seek low-cost housing in ghetto areas of the central cities. In New York City the ethnic population has been further swelled by the influx of Puerto Rican immigrants to the point where "majority groups" are outnumbered by "minorities" in the core of the region, primarily Manhattan. The educational problems produced by large concentrations of low-income residents, many of whom come from culturally deprived backgrounds, have been dramatized recently by civil rights protest movements that have been gathering momentum in places like Chicago and New York. With good reason, minority group leaders have come to view education as a significant part of the solution to their problems, and tremendous pressure has been and will continue to be placed on school administrators in an effort to upgrade the educational opportunities of such groups. The ecological concentration of Negro and other ethnic low-income groups in urban communities has made the provision of adequate educational facilities in these areas extremely difficult. Inadequate budgets, over-crowding, the reluctance of competent teachers to work in such areas, subcultural resistance on the part of the children to participation in school activities, and special educational problems such as extreme cultural deprivation, language barriers, lower health standards, and the necessity of many children to hold jobs in order to aid in sup-porting their families all have contributed to the problem of educat-ing these groups. Schools in slum areas have therefore generally been of significantly lower quality than those in middle- and upper-income areas of the city. As a result civil rights groups in Chicago and New York have suggested that total integration of the school system as a whole (for example, *no* school to have more than 50 per cent Negroes in the student body) is the only answer to the problem of providing equal educational opportunities for their members. They have furthermore demanded that total integration be undertaken immediately. Clearly the difficulties, in both financial and social terms, of implementing such a policy in an urban community having a great concentration of minority group residents are mammoth, yet it is this kind of large-scale problem with which the urban school system must grapple.

Several other major migratory movements of the American pop-ulation have taken place during the last half century that are of sig-nificance for educational policy and problems. Perhaps the most striking of these has been a westward migration that has resulted especially in the accelerating population growth of California and a corresponding decline in the rate of increase in the northeastern part of the country. During 1963 California surpassed New York as the most populous state in the Union, and demographers predict the current trend will continue for at least another decade. A mush-rooming population has placed great stresses on California's educa-tional system, and many problems remain despite the apparent will-ingness of citizens in that state to allocate large proportions of avail-able resources to the provision of educational facilities and services. In any rapidly developing area there will be many competing de-mands on local government to provide basic services for the incoming population, and consequently budgets are likely to be under greater strain than in more settled areas. At the same time the political situation is likely to be in a constant state of flux as new groups attempt to obtain a voice in local affairs and old residents struggle to hang on to positions of power in the community. In the resulting conflict between new elements and vested interests, the school system is very likely to be one of the major battlegrounds. And instability in local affairs may be reflected in educational policy and practice.

While the westward movement encompasses all population groups, a significant corresponding migration involves the selective movement of older people both to the West and to the South—primarily Florida. The development of large retirement communities in Southern California, Florida, and other areas having warm climates has implications for local school systems, since, as one would expect, this population group is less likely to take an active interest in schools and is less willing (and able) to provide adequate support for an educational system. In places where elderly persons make up a disproportionate part of the local population, therefore, obtaining tax support for schools or floating a bond issue for school construction may be more difficult.

Another selective population movement that is of significance for educational policy is the shift from farm to nonfarm areas that has resulted in a diminishing rural population in this country throughout the last fifty or sixty years. In addition to contributing greatly to the tendency toward consolidation of school districts which has already been commented upon, the farm-nonfarm shift also creates problems for city schools in providing for the adjustment or rural-born children to urban life. As the society becomes more and more urbanized, those who remain on the farm also develop special educational needs that must be met in a realistic and sophisticated way if our farm population is to remain an integral part of the society.

As members of the society have become increasingly mobile, geographically and probably socially as well, the traditional interdependence between the nuclear family (father, mother, and their children) and the extended family (grandparents, aunts, uncles, cousins, et cetera) has to some extent been weakened. As a result, in many places the importance of the role of the extended family as a socializing and culture-transmitting influence has been reduced. As has been suggested above, this has placed additional responsibilities and burdens on the school to function in place of the extended family. Systematic data are lacking here, but on theoretical grounds it might be argued that in situations where effective extended family support for the child was lacking, teachers would be more likely to become involved in playing such a role in addition to their role as mentor. This might also be true in urban environments where children often find themselves alienated from effective contact with the adult community even though the extended family group might be close by.

Some of the implications of such a development for the performance of the teacher role were discussed in the preceding chapter.

The changing technological characteristics of our culture have altered many of the occupational roles in the society, and a number of related changes have taken place in the composition of the labor force, the most important of which has been the increasing proportion of women who are employed. It is clear that automation, as well as the increase in clerical positions that has resulted from the tendency toward bureaucratization, has had a lot to do with the number of women who hold full or part-time jobs. But just as important has been the basic shift in the attitude of the society about the proper role of women and their capability to do most of the things that men can do. The educational system has contributed much to this process by providing women with the skills necessary to compete successfully with men in nearly every field of endeavor.

More students have been employed in recent years, according to Bernert and Nam (2.8 million age 14–17 in 1959), but fewer have been leaving school in order to work (2.2 million of these were still enrolled in school).[9] For the most part jobs held by students are unskilled, and the evidence is overwhelming that those who drop out of school before graduation (there were 800,000 school dropouts aged 16 and 17 in October, 1959)[10] get lower paying and lower prestige jobs than those who remain in school. In addition, the government figures reported by Bernert and Nam indicate that a quarter of those who had dropped out of school were unemployed as compared with only an eighth of the June graduates at the same time. These figures also support the view that the changing technological characteristics of our society are creating significant new responsibilities for the school. If anything, we can expect these responsibilities to become increasingly important as the composition of the labor force continues to shift.

URBANIZATION AND SUBURBANIZATION

As was pointed out above, one of the most important changes in the population structure of the United States has been the growth and development of large cities accompanied by satellite urban communities that have tended to merge with one another to form the more or less complex residential, commercial, and industrial areas now designated as metropolitan regions. The propensity of human beings to collect themselves together and form villages, towns, and cities is not a new characteristic of our species, but the extent to which this tendency has been carried in the United States and the forms of community life that have evolved as a result are unique in the history of the world. In 1960 nearly 70 per cent of the population, or more than 126 million persons, were classified as residing in urban as opposed to rural-farm and rural-nonfarm places. Furthermore, of this number, 36 million persons were living in the metropolitan regions associated with the five largest cities in the country: New York, Chicago, Los Angeles, Philadelphia, and Detroit.[11]

Dramatic increases have occurred in the size of metropolitan areas, but perhaps even more significant have been the changes that have taken place in their structure. At least in respect to the largest cities, we have apparently witnessed a reversal in the long-existent tendency for population growth to occur most rapidly at the core of the city. Instead, outlying areas have absorbed the major part of the population increase while the center city has remained relatively stable in size or has even, in some cases, undergone a decline in population. As a consequence, entire sections of the country have become essentially urban in character, as cities and eventually metropolitan regions have grown together into what the demographers are now describing as a "megalopolis." Projections of present trends indicate, for example, that by 1975 the region along the Eastern seaboard from Boston to Baltimore and Washington, D.C., will be essentially a single urban area, although pockets of open land may remain. Similar predictions have been made for an eventual linking of the metropolitan region surrounding Los Angeles with the urban complex having San Francisco as its focus.

The growth of complex urban and suburban areas has created many problems for those who must assume the responsibility for providing the residents of these communities with essential services, not to mention those things that make life easier and more productive. Coordination and planning among the many different communities involved must take place if the changes wrought by rapid population growth are not to completely disrupt local government. Transportation problems must be solved so that people can get to work (and they tend to work at increasing distances from their place of residence), taxes must be raised to pay for services, the democratic process must be served and citizens must be given a voice in local affairs, laws must be passed and enforced in order to make it possible for large numbers of diverse individuals to coexist while literally living on top of one another, and so on through the familiar maze of problems which arise whenever many people decide to settle in one place.

Urban and suburban school systems face many of the same problems encountered by other local governmental agencies, since they are typically semiautonomous political units (frequently with powers to raise their own tax revenues) and they are in the business of providing their constituents with an increasingly complex range of services requiring specialized facilities and personnel. Some of these problems—such as ensuring the availability of financial resources, the construction of adequate facilities, the recruitment of a competent teaching staff, and the establishment of effective administrative procedures to handle the increasing size and complexity of the educational system—have been examined briefly above and will be the subject of further discussion in succeeding chapters. However, because of the unique functions of educational institutions in modern society, urbanization and suburbanization have created some special problems for the school that require attention at this point. These include (1) the responsibility of the school for helping to acculturate members of the diverse groups which comprise most urban populations, (2) the increasingly important role of the school in providing support for social control· mechanisms in communities that have been characterized by high rates of violation of social norms, in part because of the lack of effective means of socializing children and subsequently enforcing normative prescriptions and proscriptions, and (3) the necessity for the school to provide special educational experiences in order to adequately prepare children for the adjustment to urban life.

THE ACCULTURATION OF IMMIGRANT AND MINORITY GROUPS

Unlike the relative homogeneity of the traditional rural community or small town, urban complexes have been characterized by the great cultural diversity of their populations. This has been due in large part to the tendency of immigrant groups (and migrants from rural areas) to settle in large cities in order to be near job markets as well as other people having similar cultural backgrounds. The result has been the formation of ethnic enclaves scattered throughout urban areas but concentrated in the central city in particular. Urban school systems have been forced to make special provisions for such groups in order to speed up the process of acculturation and contribute to the adjustment of their members to American society. Special courses in the English language and in American history and citizenship have been required, along with provisions for vocational training and guidance. In addition to difficulties in recruiting sufficient teachers who possess a facility in the languages spoken by such groups, the acculturation process is complicated by the normal resistance of ethnic groups to pressures to give up traditional ways of doing things. Although the greatest influx of immigrants was halted by restrictive legislation in the 1920's (which did not affect the rate of migration of citizens from our territories, including Puerto Rico), distinct groups still exist within each of our major cities, and urban school systems must continue to make special provision for them. Except for the removal of the language barrier, many of the individuals who are moving to northeastern and western cities from the South and rural North create many of the same special problems for the educational system. Thus the Negro who moves from rural Georgia to Chicago, New York, or Detroit must learn to adapt to a basically different culture in much the same way that the Hungarian or Chinese immigrant must adapt. In this process the educational system currently plays and will continue to play a vital role.

SOCIAL CONTROL IN URBAN AREAS

Many observers have noted the fact that urban conditions tend to decrease the effective control of the community over the behavior of its members. Due to the relatively high degree of anonymity that is characteristic of city life, informal mechanisms of social control that seem to work fairly effectively in smaller, more homogeneous communities have little impact on the behavior of most citizens (an exception would be those situations where a particular group of people have established a community enclave within the boundaries of the city—under these conditions behavior occurring *within* the community might be subject to normative regulation by the community). As a consequence of this lack of informal control, along with a number of other factors, including economic and social deprivation, cities are characterized by high rates of deviance of various sorts, ranging from the commission of criminal acts as defined by statutory law to violations of less important norms—for example, manners or modes of dress.

As an agency of social control and integration, the school is charged by society with a certain amount of responsibility in inculcating basic social norms. In urban school systems this function becomes of greater importance since the degree of normative integration of the society depends more on whether the members of the society voluntarily adhere to social norms than on the existence of strong informal controls (penalties and rewards). The situation is made more complicated by the fact that due to the cultural diversity that is typical of most cities, the school is likely to find itself in conflict with parents on many questions (or at least encounter lack of support) arising from its attempts to influence the social behavior of students. The school may then find it necessary to become involved in the normative education or re-education of parents, at best a delicate and extremely difficult task, in order to make any headway with children, since without parental support the school is likely to have little influence. This is especially true in those areas where the society recognizes the primary responsibility of the parent.

Attempts by the school to teach particular social norms and values may not always be to the benefit of the pupil or the society

as a whole. Most school personnel come from middle- and upper-
middle-class cultural backgrounds and are currently members of
social groups for which such values and norms are appropriate. The
child who must learn to live in a community that is characterized
by other than middle-class norms may not find behavior based on
such norms helpful in adjusting to the social system with which he
must deal on a daily basis. Since children typically are not free
to abandon their community and move to one better suited to them,
the child faced with a conflict between what he learns is proper
behavior at school and the way he is expected to behave at home is
in a difficult situation. He must either make a choice or attempt to
play different roles in school and at home, an alternative which is
sure to involve him in role conflict sooner or later.

ADJUSTMENT TO URBAN LIFE

Although we are beginning to realize how little we know about
the psychological and sociological effects of urban living on individuals and families, there is no doubt that urbanization has produced
striking changes in normal patterns of behavior and in the kinds of
situations and experiences with which city dwellers must deal. As
we learn more about the special abilities and skills needed by the
urbanite in order to adapt effectively to his unique social and physical
environment, the implications for educational policy will become
clearer. Some speculations are possible, however, in the absence of
research findings.

One fairly obvious conclusion concerning the curriculum of urban
schools is that it ought to provide students with the information and
skills they need to take advantage of the various resources—cultural,
economic, and social—of the place in which they live. Urban school
systems also have a special responsibility to train and motivate
students to participate actively and intelligently in local governmental
affairs and to accept their responsibilities as citizens for the welfare
of the community in the absence of external sanctions for antisocial
behavior. Perhaps more than in any other social environment, the
urban dweller must be his brother's keeper if our cities are not to
turn into jungles where order is maintained only by force of arms.
In relation to this aspect of the urban school's functions, it should
be noted that the diversity of beliefs and cultural traditions characteristic of the city makes it of critical importance for schools to put
special emphasis on increasing students' awareness, understanding,
and tolerance for the beliefs of groups other than their own.

Finally, it would appear to be worth considering the possibility
that urban schools ought to be making some conscientious attempts
to teach children something about the problems of maintaining rela-

tively stable and productive social relationships in order that, as adults living in the midst of an increasingly complicated system, they will be able to exert some measure of control over the social factors that are likely to affect their own lives.

THE NEGRO REVOLUTION

Of all of the changes that are taking place in American society at the present time, the one that has had the most dramatic and far-reaching effects on almost every aspect of the social order has been the awakening of militant Negro desires for equal status in the society. Triggered in part by the 1954 Supreme Court ruling that segregated educational facilities are inherently unequal, and fed by growing feelings of frustration as Negroes begin to perceive themselves as capable of competing on an equal footing with whites while being denied the right to do so, the dramatic increase in the intensity of Negro feeling on this issue has taken place with such speed that many members of the white community are still unwilling to fully acknowledge all that has happened.

The facts, however, cannot be ignored. Although the Negro community and its leaders are deeply divided over the path to be taken in achieving their goals, the die has been cast in a battle that is not likely to end until all vestiges of slavery have been eliminated. And every indication is that Negroes are no longer willing to wait for whites voluntarily to grant equal status. The Negro is demanding that we acknowledge his full citizenship right now, not at some distant point in the future.

As in any social movement of this kind, the evidence is that the bulk of the Negro community has thus far been only peripherally or sporadically involved in the ferment. Aside from a school boycott or two and the historic civil rights march on the Capitol, the responsibility for waging the fight has been borne by a relatively small leadership group. But the underlying support for the activities of this group is clearly present. And pressure can be expected to mount as the revolutionary contagion spreads. The nature and depth of the emotions aroused by the problem of racial prejudice and discrimination make it impossible for any Negro publicly to disengage himself from the conflict without incurring the hostility of other members of his group.

The only questions that remain concern the specific form that the revolution will take as it gathers momentum and active support from the rank and file of Negroes. The alternatives range from peaceful but persistent demonstrations of Negro demands for equal status, to the advocacy of violence where necessary in an attempt to force respect for Negro rights and, at the extreme, the repudiation by

Negroes of white society altogether (the course taken by the Black Muslim movement). It seems likely that a primary factor in determining the choice of most Negroes among these alternatives will be the willingness of white society to accede to the initial nonviolent demands of Negro leadership and the degree to which Negroes feel that sufficient progress is being made through peaceful means. As long as responsible Negro leaders can produce evidence of significant gains made without resorting to violence and excessive civil disobedience, it will be difficult for extremist elements in the Negro community to gain enough of a following to have any long-range impact. Nevertheless the presence of such elements in the background cannot be ignored. They simultaneously strengthen and make more precarious the position of moderates who must balance on the fine line between taking a tough enough stand to satisfy a militant constituency and avoiding actions that will so antagonize the white community as to negate the value of the concessions won.

Everywhere in this conflict the school is and has been a central focus of concern. The educational gains of Negroes at all levels have played an important part in their identification with the values of the dominant white culture and their resulting feelings of deep frustration when confronted with a curtailment of rights and opportunities. These frustrations, along with the manifest consequences of their impatience, can be expected to become more pronounced unless occupational and social opportunities grow apace. At the other end of the process, Negro leaders have correctly perceived the vital role of education in the future progress of Negroes as individuals and as a group. They have concentrated their efforts on ensuring the access of Negroes to formerly all-white schools, improving the "racial balance" where imbalance of either type exists, and obtaining compensatory educational facilities for "culturally deprived" Negroes in all situations.

The active interest in education on the part of civil rights leaders has already created numerous difficulties for teachers, parents, administrators, school board members, politicians, and others involved in education. The salience of the role of public education in this country makes it almost inevitable that the school will continue to be a center of controversy in the civil rights struggle as long as the conflict exists. We shall want to return to an examination of some of the specific issues in this area in subsequent sections of this book.

POLITICAL CHANGE—COMMUNITY, NATION, AND WORLD

Two major changes (that have had and will continue to have a significant impact on education) have taken place in the governmental structure of society during the last fifty years. The first of these has been the steadily increasing involvement of government in the activities of members of the society, a change which has come about as governmental agencies at all levels—federal, state, and local—have assumed greater responsibility for the management of a larger and more complex society. Not only have governments grown in size, but they have also grown in sheer power and in the number of areas over which they exert an influence—from the regulation of interstate commerce to the operation of parking meters and control over rents.

The effects of this change in government on education can be divided into two categories: direct and indirect. In the first category are included such things as state and federal financial aid to education and regulatory legislation concerned with school management and educational policies. As has been pointed out, despite the fact that the federal government has carefully avoided any attempt to change educational practice directly, federal programs of financial aid to states and other agencies for the support of a variety of educational programs, including vocational training, teacher and counselor training, tests and measurements, and educational research, have had important influences on school policies and practices. State governments have had an even more direct influence on education through regulation of the length of the school year and the establishment of certification requirements for teachers, minimum course requirements for graduation from high school, and the like. The judicial branch of the government has also had a great influence through its adjudication of a number of critical issues directly concerning the schools— for example, racial segregation and a variety of questions concerning the separation of church and state.

In addition to more or less direct effects on the schools resulting from increasing government involvement in the field of education, there is another quite different way in which the growth of government has influenced education in this country. As government has come to play a vital part in the lives of members of the society, it has become correspondingly more important for educated citizens to understand something about the workings of government, not only because the individual must deal with government agencies in the course of his daily life, but also because our particular form of government requires the participation of informed citizens in the political process itself. Thus, as governments grow in size and influence, so grows the responsibility of the school for providing new members of the society with the information necessary for them to assume their proper role in the democratic process. This is in addition to that which is necessary for them to take full advantage of the opportunities afforded by governmental policies affecting them as citizens and members of the society.

An additional indirect effect is related to government's relatively new role as a major source of employment for persons in virtually every occupational field one can imagine. The implications of government personnel policies and requirements for the educational system will be examined in more detail below, but it should be noted here that the development of more or less objective standards for hiring, and promotion by civil service agencies at all levels of government has had a tremendous impact on the occupational structure of the society and on such critical variables as opportunities for social mobility and the kinds of abilities necessary for occupational advancement. In turn, this has had important consequences for what is taught in schools and on methods used to evaluate pupils. Whatever its drawbacks, the expansion of government services has had the effect of creating a major new class of occupational positions in the society: a bureaucracy in which recruitment and advancement is based largely on merit, thereby significantly increasing the opportunities for mobility in certain segments of the society, most notably for members of ethnic and minority groups.

The second major change in the political and governmental structure of the society is the growing interdependence of all governments upon one another, not only within the confines of a given society but across international boundaries as well. This development is related to the growing number and complexity of governmental functions as well as to technologic advances that have made possible virtually effortless travel and communication throughout the world. No longer is it possible for one government agency, whether at the local, state, or international level, to act independently of other agencies on any but the most provincial of problems. The effect of these changes has been to dramatically increase the scope of the school's function to include the socialization of members of a world community as well as of our own society. The problems created by the emergence of a world political community and their relevance for educational policy and practice will be examined in Chapter VIII.

CULTURAL AND SOCIAL CHANGE

A number of theories have been offered in an effort to provide a better understanding of the dynamics of social and cultural change. In general terms these theories may be divided into those concerned with the factors that produce change and those having to do with the description of patterns of change, in an attempt to provide a basis for predictions about the future developments of societies. In the latter category we find a variety of conceptualizations of "normal" change ranging from the postulation of cyclical pattern (either around a stable base or with a growing cultural base, in which case some form of step-wise progression is visualized) to an exponential curve based on the hypothesis that an increasing cultural base will produce an accelerating rate of growth. Whatever form of change is visualized, it is fairly clear that change results from the operation of a few major factors, including the influence of innovations produced by individual members of the society, the amount of contact with other cultures, and the size of the cultural base produced by the first two factors.

We have pointed out that modern society is characterized by rapid social and cultural change that affects all parts of the society, although at varying rates. Thus far it appears that we are in a period of accelerating technological change, although it is not clear how long this can last. There can be little doubt that our present rate of change has been produced by the interactive effect of the three variables mentioned above (innovators, culture contact, and the culture base) combined with such "natural" change agents as a growing population and a plentiful supply of resources. Many anthropologists and sociologists have observed that the appearance of any innovation, whether social or technological, is the result not only of the creative imagination of the innovator but also of the relevance of the existing supply of information and techniques—the cultural base—which, in turn, is greatly influenced by contact between members of societies having different cultures. An additional factor is the degree to which members of the society devote their attention to the solving of a particular problem. Thus, we would not have predicted the invention of the atom bomb prior to Einstein's innovations in the field of mathematics and physics, or, probably, without the stimulus of World War II. The accumulation of knowledge and techniques in modern industrial society has made it possible for members of the society to work on solutions to problems that could not have been imagined as little as fifty or a hundred years ago.

The interactive nature of the culture change variables can also be emphasized by pointing out the way in which technological innovations in the fields of communication and transportation have contributed to increased culture contact throughout the world. In turn, this increased contact among members of societies having diverse beliefs, interests, and skills no doubt has played an important part in the overall process of innovation and change.

Many of the problems that are caused by social and cultural change result from the fact that all parts of the society do not change at the same rate, either because new information and techniques take longer to reach some parts of the society than others or because some groups within society hold beliefs that tend to make their members more resistant to change. To the extent that differential diffusion of change is a universal characteristic of complex societies, a continual state of tension or stress created by varying rates of change is also a characteristic. In periods of extremely rapid change, such as the one in which we currently find ourselves, we can predict that the amount of stress present will increase in proportion to increases in the rate of change. It should be noted, however, that some of the innovations that have contributed materially to our society's rapid change—namely, the growth of the mass media—have probably also has a salutory effect in facilitating the diffusion of innovations throughout the society in a way not before possible. At least with respect to some parts of the culture, television, radio, magazines, and newspapers have no doubt had the effect of reducing social tension produced by differential rates of culture change.

As we shall see in the chapters that follow, the educational system will continue to play a critical role in mediating between the culture of the society and its members. In this process the school must be both conservative and creative, a preserver of tradition and a destroyer of outdated beliefs. Because of its location along with the family at the very center of the social process, the success of the school in performing its often contradictory functions may turn out to be the factor on which the question of the ultimate survival of the society may turn. As a reflection of the society in microcosm, the educational system contains all of society's tensions, incongruities, and inconsistencies. It seems very likely that the way in which we handle our educational problems will determine to a very great extent our ability to manage our collective affairs in the broadest and most important sense.

•

CHAPTER FOUR

The School As an Agent

of

Social Control and Integration

•

Often overlooked in debates about whether social scientists will ever be able to predict human behavior is the fact that the very existence and continuity of our society is based on the ability of its members to anticipate one another's behavior with extraordinary accuracy. People do not, for the most part, behave capriciously or according to a table of random numbers. Instead, the great majority of all individual acts are performed in accordance with established social norms that are adhered to at least by other group members if not everyone in the society, and which are further routinized by individual habit patterns. The existence of normative prescriptions and proscriptions that cover most of the important aspects of human social life; combined with habitual individual variations within the socially tolerated boundaries of behavior, adds up to a highly regular and therefore predictable social order. That this is so is as it should be. Without the possibility of making relatively accurate predictions about the behavior of our fellow citizens most of the time, life would be a hazardous enterprise. Not only would it be dangerous to perform such simple acts as crossing streets (or, for that matter, driving on them), but without the delicate fabric of formal and informal controls over individual initiative and whim the entire political and social structure of the society would be seriously threatened.

A well-integrated and smoothly functioning society, especially one characterized by rapid technological and social change, depends on an exceptionally high degree of agreement among its members about basic norms and values. Members of the society must also have acquired the social skills necessary for them to perform effectively the occupational, familial, and other roles which they will have to play as a result of their various positions in the social order. In addition, it is important to recognize that the socialization process involves more than the learning of table manners, rules about correct procedures for filing one's income tax, or the behavior expected of someone occupying the positions of husband and father. Even more basic to effective social interaction at the group or the societal level is the ability of individuals to empathize with members of their social group: to "take the role of other" in viewing their own behavior from the standpoint of those with whom they are dealing as well as to predict how others will behave. In terms suggested by George Herbert Mead, the encouragement of individuals in the development of an adequate "social self"[1] is an important aspect of the processes leading to a society characterized by relatively conflict-free and productive social interactions.

It may be hypothesized that as a society undergoes rapid social change the importance of this latter aspect of the socialization process increases due to a relative decrease in the stability and effectiveness of traditional norms and values. Thus effective interaction is likely to depend more on the empathic capabilities of group members where there is a relatively undefined and diffuse normative structure than in situations where norms are clearly defined. We shall want to return to this point below.

As one of several important agencies mediating between the individual and the society, the school helps to transmit social norms and values as well as the techniques by which the individual is able to anticipate accurately the behavior of other members of the society. Indeed, as we have indicated, the primary function of the school in the society is the inculcation of a cultural heritage which is made up of norms and values as well as accumulated information and skills. In fulfilling its function as a socializing agent, the school, along with the family, plays an important role in reinforcing the normative integration of the society. It is clear that the degree to which the school accomplishes this task effectively and in harmony with other socializing influences is a significant factor in the subsequent adjustment of individuals to the society and in the functioning of the society as a whole.

MEANS BY WHICH THE SCHOOL FACILITATES SOCIALIZATION

Before turning to an examination of the special problems that a rapidly changing society creates for the school in fulfilling its social control function, some consideration must be given to the various mechanisms by which the school contributes to the process of socialization and thereby to the stability of the society. Categorization is not always easy or perfect, but a rough distinction can be made among four different means by which the school aids in socializing new members of the society. These include the following: (1) the transmission of culture, including norms, values, and information, through direct teaching: (2) the establishment of social groups in which children have an opportunity to acquire various social skills, (3) the provision of significant other individuals (teachers, counselors, et cetera) who can serve as supplementary adult role models for students, and (4) the use of both negative and positive sanctions to reinforce socially acceptable behavior on the part of children.

THE TRANSMISSION OF CULTURE

The importance of the school's function in helping to transmit a cultural heritage from one generation to the next was discussed in some detail in an earlier chapter. It should be noted that it is precisely here that the conflict between the school's orientation toward the past and its responsibility to the future is most sharply drawn. This can be seen in the frequently ambivalent attitude of educators toward the teaching of ancient history or classical languages such as Latin and Greek as opposed to science, mathematics, or the social sciences. The problem of relative emphasis between classical and modern subjects in elementary and secondary school curricula has been debated by educators and academicians for some time. Although many scholars have stressed the importance of a firm grounding in the classics, the trend appears to favor strongly the teaching of an increasingly present- and future-oriented curriculum. A facility in Latin is no longer required for admission to college in this country, and both literature and history courses are likely to accent the events and accomplishments of modern times. It seems plausible that a continued decrease in the familiarity of a substantial proportion of the members of society with the cultural roots of our social order will tend to accentuate our accelerating rate of social and cultural change.

In connection with the transmission of culture it should be pointed out that the school also contributes to the stability of the society by preparing its citizens to participate intelligently in the political process, a teaching function which in many ways helps to bridge the gap between the old and the new. In addition to being able to read, write, and comprehend current events, members of the society must also have some understanding of how our political system works, including an appreciation of the fundamental principles underlying the specific governmental forms that are unique to American society. In this respect the study of recent history and a knowledge of current practices and problems are of equal importance from an educational standpoint. The responsibility of the school to provide both kinds of learning experiences for its students is clear.

In addition to formal instruction in history, civics, and political science, students also may learn a great deal about politics through participation in student governmental activities in school or college. Although the structure and effectiveness of student governments varies considerably from institution to institution, this aspect of extracurricular activity in many schools provides students with a unique introduction to the political process—from the power of the vote (and the voter) to the frequent frustrations inherent in a democratic system. Because of its semi-official status in the normal activities of most schools and its relationship to both the formal and informal socializing functions of the school, consideration of the importance of student government leads directly into a discussion of the second important mechanism by which schools influence the degree of social control and integration in the society: the facilitation of the acquisition of social skills by children through participation in the informal social system of the school.

THE SCHOOL AS A CONTEXT FOR SOCIAL INTERACTION

A major source of controversy in current debates over the proper functions of the school relates to whether the school ought to concern itself with the social adjustment of its pupils as an integral part of its contribution to the process of socialization. The reaction of many critics of our educational system following Sputnick was that we have been spending too much time on activities that fall under the general heading of "life adjustment" courses and not nearly enough on hard core academic subject matter.[2] Particularly at the elementary level it is probably true that some schools had gone overboard in their concern for pupil adjustment, the result being that less attention was given to instruction in reading, mathematics, history, and the like. On the other hand, it should be recognized that *whether or not* any specific attention is paid to this aspect of the socialization process by teachers or administrators, a major part of what children learn in school falls under the heading of the acquisition of social skills.

Most parents are aware of the fact that the social groups to which a child belongs have a great influence on his behavior. Children acquire many of the interactional skills they will use throughout their life in the context of the social groups formed during childhood and adolescence. Omar K. Moore has suggested that a successful outcome to the socialization process depends on the individual having an opportunity to try out alternative ways of behaving in various situations without suffering serious penalties for mistakes.[3] The peer group can provide a setting in which the child can experiment with different behaviors without fear of serious reprisals (such as being thrown out of the group) unless, of course, he fails to recognize the group's milder signals of disapproval when he commits an inappropriate act. The typical activities of most adolescent and childhood groups, including games and other role-playing activities, are especially appropriate socialization devices for three reasons: they can be enjoyed for their own sake (as opposed to being a means to some other end), they require their participants to master skills that will be useful in handling the more serious interactional problems their participants will encounter as adult members of the society, and they contain no serious penalties for errors.[4]

These socializing activities (Moore calls them "autotelic folk models") have an additional important characteristic. They contain rules according to which the behavior of the participants must conform if they wish to take part. Just as the society in which the adult participates has rules, so does the game that is played by the neighborhood gang or, at a different level of analysis, the informal social system of the classroom. Furthermore, Moore hypothesizes that the factor that determines the usefulness of the autotelic activity in facilitating the process of socialization is the degree to which its rules are similar in structure to the rules of that aspect of social behavior for which it is presumed to be relevant. It is attention to the normative structure of the activity (and the recognition of its existence) that differentiates this approach from a number of earlier conceptualizations of the part played by the interactional systems of children and what goes on in them. It is likely that many of the problems encountered by administrators who attempted unsuccessfully to make use of principles of the progressive movement in education were the result of a failure to perceive the difference between freedom to experiment within a carefully constructed normative framework (for example, one that focuses the child's activity on the important problems) and freedom resulting from an absence of rules altogether.

Looked at from this standpoint, many of the activities in which children engage apart from their formal work in the classroom have direct relevance to the socialization process. To the extent that the school is charged with any responsibility for socialization beyond the inculcation of factual knowledge and intellectual skills, it would appear to be appropriate for administrators and teachers to take cognizance of the part played by peer groups and especially the characteristics of the activities that take place in them. As we learn more about the dynamics of various aspects of the socialization process, it may turn out that important gains could be made by manipulating the structure of informal groups within the school and by encouraging students to participate in activities designed to maximize their opportunities to acquire useful interactional skills.

Because of the importance of Omar Moore's insights into the nature of socialization and their implications for educational practice, we shall want to return to an examination of his approach in the context of our discussion of the role of the school in contributing to innovation in the society. The following chapter's discussion may be anticipated here, however, by noting that what Moore suggests about the kinds of mechanisms that play an important role in facilitating the acquisition of social skills may be applied to the teaching of more legitimate cognitive and intellectual skills with particularly interesting and provocative conclusions. Among other things, Moore has been experimenting with techniques for teaching children to read that are based on his notions about the importance of autotelic activities in the learning process. At this stage his findings appear to be well worth the serious consideration of educators who are under increasing pressure to satisfy both the groups that want the school to take on more responsibility for turning out well-adjusted citizens and those who are pressing for an upgrading in the traditional subjects.

An additional significant implication of the influence of informal interaction within the school on the socialization of students relates to the problem of racial integration. Most leaders of the civil rights movement are aware of the fact that the educational process involves more than the acquisition of simple intellectual skills. For this reason they have been unwilling to settle for educational reforms that do not alter the basic social structure of the school system, particularly in areas where ecological concentrations of nonwhite groups have produced *de facto* segregation in the schools. They recognize that unless Negro and other minority group members have an opportunity to interact informally on a daily basis with children from middle- and upper-middle-class white families, the Negro child has little chance to acquire the social skills and midde-class values that will make it possible for him to move into these groups as an adult, even assuming that arbitrary barriers to Negro participation have been removed. The boundaries of the school's responsibility in this area remain to be clearly specified. Nevertheless, we can anticipate increasing minority group pressures on school boards and administrators to do away with the traditional neighborhood school wherever high concentrations of low income individuals and minority group members have produced a unique subculture that is perpetuated through informal interactional processes in neighborhood schools.

THE PROVISION OF ROLE MODELS

The third major way in which the school contributes to the socialization of new members of the society is through the impact of school personnel—mainly teachers but also counselors and occasionally principals and others—who serve as role models for students in the same way that parents provide examples for their children to emulate. The process by which the child (or for that matter, the adult) identifies with *significant other individuals* in his "life space" is both conscious and unconscious. Their influence on his behavior may range from manner of speech and dress to the formation of basic values and beliefs. Since most behavior and much of learning take place in groups, it is not surprising that a significant proportion of an individual's attitudes, beliefs, and habitual ways of doing things are shaped by a relatively small number of significant others who for each individual provide the frame of reference through which each individual views the world. Because of their special relationship to the individual, each significant other plays an important part in defining (and enforcing) habitual ways of responding to the social environment and in establishing standards against which the individual evaluates the behavior of those with whom he must deal.

In many respects the related processes of personality development and socialization may be described entirely in terms of the more or less constantly changing set of significant others or reference figures that serve to orient the individual in relation to his social system. As the child grows up, his maturation is marked by the adoption of new reference individuals and the abandonment of existing figures, though some persons—for example, parents, older siblings, and intimate friends—are likely to serve as reference figures throughout the individual's life. The socialization process continues beyond the period of formal schooling, and adult socialization also is based in large part on the acquisition of new reference figures as the individual moves into new social groups.

Because of his legitimate and formally defined relationship to students, the teacher can seldom avoid becoming a significant reference figure for them, at least for a short period of time. The fact that the relationship between teacher and student is temporary means that in the long run the influence of any one teacher on a child is likely to be of less importance than that of individuals with whom the child is in continuing contact, like parents or brothers and sisters. But there have been many notable exceptions to this rule, cases in which teachers have made lifelong impressions on their students and have helped to set standards for them that have remained relevant and important long after contact between teacher and student had been lost.

The nature of the teacher-student relationship has a great deal to do with the universality of this influence process. The characteristics of the teacher's personality and background as well as the needs, interests, and capabilities of the student will determine to a large extent the degree to which the student tends to adopt his teacher as a role model and what the precise nature of the teacher's influence on the student will be. Up to now social scientists have not been able to learn very much about the dynamics of this process of identification beyond the knowledge that some of the important factors in the equation are the interest that the teacher takes in the student, the degree to which the teacher is able to empathize with the needs of the student, and the general leadership qualities of the teacher, including the energy with which he exploits the opportunities afforded by his position to command respect as well as obedience. As we strive to increase our understanding of the teaching-learning process, more systematic attention will have to be given to the variables affecting the quality of the relationship between the teacher and his student.

Because most parents are aware of the potential impact of teachers on their children, a great deal of community interest is usually focused on the teacher selection process and on the kind of individuals who are recruited to teach in the schools. While it is to be expected that parents will be concerned about whom their children adopt as a role model, even for a short time, their concern often creates a conflict between objective criteria of competence to perform the teaching function (as defined by the formal specifications and requirements of the job) and parental judgments about the possible harmful consequences of allowing a person with socially unacceptable beliefs or attitudes to occupy a position of such influence regardless of his academic qualifications. Thus while the teacher role may be formally specific in its content, the impact of the teacher on the student often extends beyond this specific content. Recognition of this fact has on many occasions produced sharp disagreement among parents, administrators, and teachers about recruitment and advancement policies.

Middle-class groups exert a controlling influence over much of educational policy-making in this country. Parental concern about the influence of teachers on their children is reflected in the fact that the majority of public school teachers (as well as administrators) come from a middle- or upper-middle-class background. Consequently there is a strong tendency for teachers to pass on middle-class value orientations and beliefs to their students. This no doubt has a reinforcing effect on the stability of the social system as a whole, but as we have suggested previously, it also creates some problems for children who must live in social groups characterized by norms and values differing from those held by their middle-class teachers. It may also make it necessary for the child to choose between identification with his parents and identification with his teachers, a situation that no matter how resolved works against the educational process by destroying the necessary complementary and supportive relationship between teacher and parents. Furthermore, to the extent that the values inherent in the new adolescent society are at variance with existing middle-class value orientations, the stage is set for conflict between teachers and students as a group. This conflict may be reflected in a lack of student commitment to the educational process (as Coleman has indicated) or, if some pupils do become involved in learning, their potential alienation from the peer group. Because of their particular relevance to the consideration of the impact of change on the educational system, we shall return to a consideration of these issues in the second part of this chapter.

SOCIALIZATION AND SCHOOL SANCTIONS

Finally, the school makes use of a variety of penalties and rewards to reinforce socially acceptable behavior on the part of students within the context of school activities. In the process it contributes in large measure to the socialization of students by introducing them, probably for the first time, to institutionalized mechanisms of control over individual behavior in a formal organization. Among the many different positive sanctions or rewards used by the school to induce students to act in accordance with both formal and informal school rules and regulations are school awards such as honor society membership, grades, and a variety of special privileges ranging from permission to participate in desirable extra-curricular activities to freedom from some of the rules to which these privileges are designed to ensure adherance. On the negative side, teachers may detain students at the end of the school day for bad behavior (the increasing number of students who travel to school by bus has created some problems in this respect, but many schools have solved them by setting aside one or two days a week when a special late bus is available for children who have been detained), privileges may be revoked, parents may be sent for, and, as a last resort, suspension or expulsion from school may be threatened.

Most of the techniques by which the school attempts to enforce its rules and maintain order among students parallel similar mechanisms in any formally organized group (as well as many informal groups), although typically a much greater amount of leeway is permitted in schools than is likely to be the case in other groups to which the individual will belong as an adult member of the society. The school has an important function in helping children to adjust to the strictures of formal rules and regulations concerning their behavior, while at the same time retaining some of the characteristics of the informal family group in which considerable deviance is usually allowed (it should not be concluded that there are no mechanisms of control over members' behavior in the family).

The problems of discipline and control over student behavior are frequently major areas of both administrative and teacher concern, primarily as a result of the nature of educational institutions and their relation to the society they serve. From a sociological standpoint one of the important characteristics of any social group or organization is the basis on which its members are recruited or admitted. Quite different predictions may be made, for example, about the operation of a group whose members pay to belong (such as a club, hospital, private school, or college) as opposed to an organization that pays its members to participate in its activities (a corporation or government agency). Public schools (along with a few other organizations, including penal institutions and mental hospitals) are unique in that an important segment of membership (students) neither pay nor are paid for their participation (except indirectly through parents' tax contribution) and, in addition, have no choice about whether they will participate or not. The result is a significant weakening of organizational sanctions and, consequently, of the normative structure of the group as a whole. The threat of expulsion, for example, the most extreme of the penalties any group can apply, is likely to have considerably less force in the case of a captive school population. In addition, because of the responsibility of the school to the society, it can only be used in extreme cases.

Schools, of course, vary considerably in the degree to which they are able effectively to regulate the behavior of their pupils. And within schools some teachers are able to exert much greater disciplinary influence than others. A distinction must be made, however, between pupil adherance to rules that is the result of strong institutionalized norms along with organizational sanctions that are sufficiently powerful to assure the compliance of all group members, and discipline that is based on the personal leadership qualities (and individual sanctions) of teachers and administrators. There is a difference between obedience based on the desire to please a particular teacher (or the fear of his wrath) and obedience because one is anxious to be permitted to continue to participate in the group's activities or perhaps to be given a larger share in those activities. In part this distinction helps to explain the difference between the attitudes toward education held by the first-year college student and the same student's attitudes a year earlier in high school (some additional factors such as maturation also can be discerned in this transformation).

It may also provide part of the explanation for the varying attitudes about education that are held by members of different class groups in the society and the differential degrees to which children from these various groups create discipline problems for administrators and teachers. To the extent that parents of middle- and upper-class children perceive themselves to be more heavily involved in formal educational processes, both financially and in terms of their participation in the planning and execution of school programs, this involvement is likely to be reflected in a tendency to stimulate a greater interest and participation on the part of their children. These propositions suggest that one way of raising the level of student motivation and improving discipline within the school is to increase the stake that both parents and pupils have in the outcome of the educational process. Although this may not be easy to accomplish in all circumstances, our greatest efforts along this line should be directed specifically at those groups that heretofore have not had much opportunity or inclination to participate in education at any level.

SOCIAL CHANGE AND THE SOCIALIZATION PROCESS—NORMS AND VALUES

In a society characterized by little or no social change, the task of the school in helping to socialize new members of the society is relatively simple. There is likely to be little disagreement about the content of social norms and values or about how the society is organized (or *should* be organized), including the nature and operation of its political institutions. Consequently, educators must concern themselves only with finding answers to the question of how best to instruct their pupils in order to assure their maximum conformity to established and accepted modes of behavior.

In a changing society, on the other hand, the socialization process becomes infinitely more complex. Not only are social norms and values often subject to debate by adult members of the society, but even when agreement is reached there is always the possibility that by the time the current generation of school children has reached maturity changes in the technological and social structure of the society will have forced revisions of social mores or political processes and ideologies.

THE NECESSITY FOR FLEXIBILITY IN THE SOCIALIZATION PROCESS

The socialization of new members of a changing society requires a much greater degree of flexibility on the part of the socializing agent in order to take into account current inconsistencies in the normative fabric of the society and to make allowances for future changes in what is considered to be acceptable behavior on the part of its citizens. At the same time, too quick a recognition of the possible instability of social norms is certain to reinforce existing tendencies toward normative change and may lead in the long run to social disorganization. Under conditions of rapid social and technological change, the school must strike a delicate balance between inculcating a rigid set of social norms and values that may turn out to be incompatible with changing behavior patterns on the one hand and failing to provide children with any meaningful set of normative standards that will enable them to function as well-adjusted members of the society on the other.

It is fairly clear that there are real dangers for the society on either side of this point of balance. An inflexible normative structure that is reinforced by rigid socialization practices on the part of the family and the school can be expected either to have the effect of stifling innovation or, in the event that change does take place (perhaps as a result of external influences), of putting severe strain on the society by involving individuals in conflict situations. In anthropological terms this may be described as the problem of *cultural lag* (where one part of culture—for example, technology—changes more rapidly than another part). Examples of cultural lag can be seen in many communities in the United States and in other societies throughout the world where changes introduced as a result of colonization or culture contact have placed great stress on traditional norms and values. The resistance of southern communities to the pressures produced by the ending of racial segregation provides a good example of the conflict that is induced both from the standpoint of the individual and the society when rigidly held norms are threatened by change.

Where change is introduced into situations characterized by relatively rigid norms and inflexible socialization practices, a real breakdown in the normative integration of the society may occur unless some kind of decompression mechanism can be provided to reduce gradually the incompatibility between the old normative structure and the demands of change. The alternative to gradual modification of social norms and values appears to be the complete dissolution of existing norms resulting in a chaotic and anomic (normless) state in which the absence of normative integration reinforces itself and may lead to even greater change (the phenomenon of revolution and counter-revolution). Paradoxically, from this standpoint it would appear that the society which provides for maximally efficient socialization (when narrowly defined in terms of the inculcation of existing norms) of its members may not in the long run be able to adapt easily to social and technological change (unless special care is taken to establish specific norms relating to the process of adaptation and change itself). Most highly stable primitive societies would fall into such a category, and we have evidence of the havoc that has often been wrought by the introduction of modern technology and customs into such a culture.

On the basis of what we know about the rate of social change in the United States, it may be predicted that schools (and perhaps families as well) will attempt to strike a balance between stricter socialization practices on the one hand and abdication of their responsibilities for the transmission of social norms and values on the other by shifting their focus from the specific to the general, from the inculcation of particular norms to the teaching of basic values and principles. For example, instead of trying strictly to enforce current normative proscriptions relating to socially acceptable relationships between boys and girls, educational institutions are more likely to concentrate on helping young people to understand and appreciate some of the more fundamental social values on which specific sexual norms and practices are based. In moving in this direction, educators as well as parents are likely to acknowledge the existence of strong pressures toward change. They will be permitted to have an influence on specific norms, but only within the context of a more stable general value system. Parents and educators alike will have to come to grips with the fact that the choice may lie between acceptance of the inevitability of some normative change and the complete inability of the school to influence the outcome of the socialization process.

In situations where the socializing agent (whether parent or teacher) attempts to induce the child to conform to inappropriate normative standards, the overall authority of the teacher or parent (and hence his effectiveness as a socializing agent) is threatened, particularly where the child perceives the irrationality of his elder's demands. In a context in which rationality is highly valued, the degree to which individual adults are likely to serve as significant role models for new members of the society will bear an increasingly close relationship to the reasonableness and consistency of the specific demands they make on the children involved.

THE IMPACT OF CULTURAL RELATIVITY

The introduction of a certain amount of flexibility into the socialization process would appear to be a necessary outgrowth of a rapidly changing society if the rate of innovation and development is not to be sharply curtailed. However as we have indicated, the weakening of the normative structure of the society, whether intentional or unintentional, is clearly threatening to the long-term stability of the social system and is likely to create important problems in the short run. A major danger lies in the possibility that a lessening of the strictness with which specific norms are enforced may lead to changes in the attitudes of members of the society about the legitimacy of social norms in general and consequently to an increase in the occurrence of deviant behavior of all types.

Evidence that tendencies in this direction exist in our society can be provided in the form of statistics showing increasing rates of divorce, alcoholism, drug addiction, homosexuality, and various types of crime; as well as in such informal examples as the reports of parents and educators regarding changing patterns of sexual behavior on the part of adolescents, all of which indicate a trend toward greater freedom from traditional normative standards. The process of culture change and the related weakening of social norms has no doubt been strongly influenced by the rapid development of better means of communication among the various nations and societies throughout the world. This has resulted in the realization that social norms vary greatly from society to society and that many of the beliefs and practices that have long been revered in our country are the exception and not necessarily the rule in other places. While most members of the society have not gone so far as to conclude that any practice could be justified on the grounds that an example of a society in which it was acceptable could probably be found (the doctrine of cultural relativity is more properly interpreted as referring to the fact that any aspect of the behavior of members of other societies can only be understood when it is examined in the light of their culture as a whole), it is nevertheless fairly clear that the puncture of our own isolationist bubble has contributed materially to the tendency for members of the society to take traditional social norms less seriously.

In itself, the recognition that there are other ways of doing things is probably worthwhile in making it possible for members of the society to deal objectively with the society in which they live. On the other hand, it is of critical importance that this capability for examining our own customs "in the cold light of day" does not lead us to a rejection of the legitimacy of social norms in general or to lose sight of the importance of the normative integration of society in particular.

EDUCATIONAL ALTERNATIVES

From the standpoint of educational practice, the preceding points raise important questions concerning what the school might do to help reconcile the apparent conflict between the relativity of social norms and the necessity for a certain amount of social control.

One approach might be to develop course materials for secondary school students that would enable them to gain an appreciation of the important characteristics of social systems, both in a cross-cultural context and with specific reference to our society. In providing such materials, however, it would be of special importance to emphasize the interrelationships among specific social norms and the significant role of legitimate social control mechanisms in assuring the continuity and stability of any group. In addition, the mutually dependent relationship between the individual and his social group should be considered in order to make it possible for the student to evaluate his own behavior in terms of its impact on the groups to which he belongs as well as the wider society. Increased knowledge on the part of individuals about the fundamental properties of social systems and groups combined with a greater emphasis on the underlying values of American society might serve to bridge the gap between technological change and normative rigidity that threatens the continuity and continued development of the society.

TECHNOLOGY AND NORMATIVE CHANGE

It has been noted that all parts of a culture do not change at the same rate or with the same frequency and that part of the difficulty in adapting to technological innovation, population growth or decline, or some other forms of change is this variability in the susceptibility of different parts of the culture to alteration. An interesting and important question which may be asked, therefore, about a society that is undergoing change concerns what aspects of culture are most likely to be affected first and, consequently, where points of strain between the old and the new can be discerned. It is apparent that answers to such a question have a direct bearing on the nature of the problems the school is likely to face in fulfilling its social control function through its role in the socialization process.

A major source of culture change in American society is, as we have already indicated, an unprecedented rate of technological innovation. We may predict that many of the most significant changes in the normative structure of the society will take place in those areas of culture that are most closely related to technology and, more specifically, in those aspects of the society's technology that are undergoing rapid change. To consider two specific innovations that have had a profound effect on the society, the school must deal with dramatic changes in social norms that have been produced at least in part by the development of television and the automobile.

The growth of television during the last fifteen years has had a marked impact on the behavior patterns of a large segment of the

American population and in particular on young people. Not only has the use of leisure time by both adolescents and children been greatly affected, thus altering the educational process directly through its impact on study habits and indirectly through changes in attitudes about intellectual activities, but television (much more than radio) has also had the effect of greatly expanding the "life space" of new members of the society. It has made it possible for them to participate vicariously in the activities of many different groups outside their own social environment. As a result the range of possible reference figures with whom young people can identify has been expanded enormously. Schools must now face the fact that they are competing in their attempts to transmit social norms not only with the child's family but with a host of additional socializing influences that may or may not be congruent with local values. It is fairly clear that the greater the number of influences involved in the socialization process, the greater is the likelihood that conflict among norms and values will be encountered. Television also has the effect of reinforcing the awareness on the part of children and especially adolescents that considerable disagreement exists among adults about certain of the normative prescriptions and proscriptions of the society (thereby adding to feelings of uncertainty about the legitimacy of norms). Finally, the spread of the mass media, including television, increases the vulnerability of the teacher (not to mention the parent) as an expert on all manner of subjects, thereby reducing his authority and potential influence as a socializing agent.

In a somewhat different way the development and widespread use of the automobile has also had an important impact on behavior patterns and norms in American society, particularly in regard to facilitating the growth of a separate adolescent culture. The automobile has given the teenager a degree of freedom and mobility that is quite probably unique in the history of the world. Not only has it now become possible for young people to escape almost entirely from the direct supervision of their parents, but the automobile has also given the adolescent a degree of privacy that has not before been available to him, at least in complex, industrial, or pre-industrial societies characterized by large concentrations of population. The effect of the automobile on the sexual mores of young people has been commented on by parents, educators, and others although this has always been an area in which sound data on which to base conclusions are hard to come by. There is little doubt, however, that norms relating to sexual practices in our society have been changing, and it is not unrealistic to attribute a share of the stimulus behind these changes to technological developments such as the automobile that have provided greater opportunities for sexual experimentation on the part of young people.

THE DEVELOPMENT OF ADOLESCENT SUBCULTURES

The relative freedom of the adolescent in conjunction with the practice of extending his psychological and social dependence on adults past the point of physical dependency (by prolonging the educational process) has led to the development of an increasingly well-formed teenage subculture based in large part on the rejection of the adult world and its restricting norms, values, and responsibilities, but at the same time on aspirations to achieve equal status with adults. The high school, and to an even greater extent the college, in attempting to fulfill their function in preparing young people to assume positions as responsible and well-socialized members of the society, frequently are placed in the difficult position of attempting to impose adult standards of behavior on adolescents while simultaneously rejecting their demands for equal status.

Where family support for the activities of the school is weak, where there is little relationship between what is being taught and the realistic occupational needs of students, and especially if the high school is perceived by students as the end of formal schooling, the conflict between adolescent norms and school goals may have the effect of undermining the educational process, leaving the school to function essentially as a custodial institution. A number of sociologists have made note of the fact that when this happens those who are responsible for maintaining order in the organization, whether it be a school, mental hospital, or prison, frequently resort to supporting the subculture of the inmate or client group in return for their cooperation in adhering to a minimum set of rules and regulations. Thus in such schools the teacher is likely to permit or even encourage the formation of an adolescent subculture, even one that is based on norms and values that conflict with the goals of the school, in order to keep control over his class.

Even where a high proportion of students go on to college, the growing independence of young people is reflected in behavior patterns that frequently conflict with the norms and values of the wider society and more specifically with the goals of the school. In the schools studied by James Coleman in his research on adolescent society, only a small percentage of the total number of students reported that getting good grades or being intelligent was of any particular importance for getting into the most prestigious student groups.[5] Although there was considerable variation from school to school in Coleman's sample, and while getting good grades usually carried some social advantages, it was clear that the general orientation of the adolescent society was toward nonacademic activities (for example athletics and dating) for both boys and girls. In such situations it does not seem likely that teachers could have a very great impact on pupils in terms of setting standards or in acting as significant reference figures except in individual ·cases. Coleman found, for example, that when students were asked whether their teacher's, parents', or friends' disapproval would be hardest to take as a consequence of a decision on their part to join a particular club, only 3 per cent replied that their teacher's disapproval would be of greatest importance to them, while judgments between parents and friends split the remaining 97 per cent about evenly.[6]

We may conclude that the school faces some difficult problems both in motivating students to take an interest in intellectual activities and in transmitting adult norms and values that are in conflict with those of the adolescent society. Because of the differences between middle-class beliefs and values of teachers and the normative orientations of students resulting from their allegiance to an adolescent subculture (which is often given a special twist by a different racial or ethnic background), teachers are often ineffective in fulfilling their functions as socializing agents. By attempting to influence their students they may even generate hostility toward the dominant value orientations of the society which they represent.

At the same time, as the normative integration of the society is threatened by change and the socializing influence of the family is likewise reduced as a consequence of social, demographic, and technological change, the potential importance of the school in contributing to the process of socialization is greatly enhanced. It seems clear that if the school is to do a better job in regard to socialization the emphasis will have to be shifted in the direction of basic values as opposed to specific norms, greater parental involvement in the educational process will be necessary, and in addition, something will have to be done to increase the salience of educational goals for members of the adolescent society.

TRANSMISSION OF FORMAL RULES AND TRADITIONS

The continuity of a complex society such as ours requires more than agreement among its members on a set of common norms, values, and traditional ways of behaving. As American society has grown in size and cultural complexity, political institutions have taken on an increasing number of functions, partly in response to demands for more governmental services and partly as a result of inherent organizational tendencies toward bureaucratization and increased size. The change in the importance of governmental activities at all levels, from local to national and international, has created two additional problems for our educational system that are of great concern to both educators and those who are charged with responsibility for the management of our political institutions.

The first of these relates to the question of how the school can best prepare new members of the society to assume their individual and collective responsibilities as private citizens to participate actively and intelligently in the formation of public policy. And secondly, the school must deal with the task of providing a growing number of future government officials with the intellectual skills necessary for them to deal with increasingly complex and difficult problems in situations where a mistake (or a correct decision) is likely to have far-reaching consequences.

The importance of the teaching of history, civics, and other subjects that are vital for the appreciation of our political heritage and current practices has often been overlooked in recent years. The public and professional clamor for more science and mathematics instruction following the first Soviet space achievements tended to divert the attention of those involved in the management of our schools away from this aspect of the school's functions. However, the obligation of the school to concern itself with instructing children in the workings of government as well as the values that underlie our political institutions is more salient than ever. As Vincent Ostrom has put it, "It is not possible to contemplate an advanced civilization without both a sophisticated educational system and a sophisticated political system. Jefferson once wrote, 'If a nation expects to be ignorant and free, in a state of civilization, it expects what never was and never will be.'"[7] Further, as the sheer size of government and its role in society increases, the responsibility of citizens to exercise control over it increases rather than decreases. According to Fred M. Newmann, "With increasing complexity of public issues, a population too large for mass participation in the formation of policy, and a period of time between election that gives leaders and representatives substantial leeway, the power that one delegates by voting has reached enormous proportions. As the operations of government exert potentially more control over individual behavior, so increases the amount of power that one delegates when choosing the leaders that guide such control. *By consenting to delegate magnified power, one magnifies the influence of the consent process itself.*"[8]

The dependence of a democratic government on the intelligent participation of citizens, particularly in a world that is undergoing social and political changes that daily produce new problems for our representatives in the government to solve, has been demonstrated by past successes and failures both in our society and abroad. However it is not readily apparent to what extent schools are presently contributing to the training of well-informed citizens. One study indicated, for example, that the completion of high school courses in civics or United States government is *not* related to a

belief in the freedoms guaranteed by the Constitution, that a significant segment of high school seniors do *not* agree with the freedoms
specified in the Bill of Rights, and that those students who are
most likely to *reject* democratic propositions tend to be *both* authoritarian and to classify themselves as the best supporters of American
democracy.[9]

In the face of strong external pressures from competing political
ideologies and a strong undercurrent of skepticism at home about
the wisdom of allowing the present trend toward a bigger and more
powerful central government to continue, it is of particular importance that attention be given to how the school might better fulfill
its function in this area. It is likely that some basically new
approaches to civics education will be necessary if any real progress is to be made. The work of James Coleman at the Johns Hopkins
University in the development of political games as teaching devices
would appear to be a particularly promising way of attacking the
problem, both from a pedagogical and a political standpoint. One
such new game was used by Coleman and his associates in conjunction with the 1960 election.

> A sample of voters was interviewed to determine their
> attitudes toward various issues. Then processes by which
> these attitudes could affect vote intentions were programmed
> on an electric computer. A class was divided into two sets
> of campaign strategies (a "Nixon team" and a "Kennedy
> team") and each team made campaign decisions in an
> attempt to influence the electorate. These decisions were fed
> into the computer, which gave back preliminary vote inten-
> tions. New decisions were made, and the consequences
> assessed. After a fixed number of decisions, the campaign
> was ended and the candidate with the most votes was the
> winner.[10]

Coleman reports that in one use of this game the class learned far
more about election processes than in previous courses using ordinary
techniques. In addition, student involvement in the activity was far
greater than in conventional learning situations. A particular advantage of Coleman's work is that by utilizing a role-playing technique
in which the student is forced to deal with real problems in situations that may be designed to simulate the kinds of actual variation
the decision-maker in government must handle, attention can be
concentrated on the general strategies of problem solving as opposed
to rote learning of specific procedures that may have become outdated by the time the student is ready to apply them.

Since it is unrealistic to expect any sharp reduction in the role of government in the ongoing activities of our society during the foreseeable future (indeed, quite the opposite prediction may be made with a fair degree of confidence), it may be hypothesized that one of the important factors in the continued success of our educational system will be its capacity to provide a constant supply of individuals who are not only well-trained, able, and of high integrity but who are also willing to take on the task of running our governments; local, state, and national. Thus, in addition to its training function, the school must also play a part in motivating young people to contribute their talents in the public service.

In the light of the current public image of government officials and politicians, as well as the competition for competent manpower in all sectors of the society, this will not be an easy task. Closer attention on the part of educators to the challenges, rewards, and opportunities in government will certainly be necessary if any progress is to be made. But most important, schools must find ways of increasing young people's social consciousness and sense of obligation to the society, regardless of their occupational inclinations. It is this acceptance by its citizens of mutual responsibility for the welfare of the society that provides a major key to the achievement of both progress and stability in a society such as ours. In the following chapter we shall turn to a consideration of some of the ways in which the school contributes to change and the problems that this dimension of the school's role creates for administrators, teachers, and students.

•

CHAPTER FIVE

The School As an Agent

of

Innovation and Change

•

A major theme of this book has been the inherent conflict between the role of educational institutions as transmitters of a cultural tradition—essentially a conservative function—and their responsibility to a society that has adopted innovation and change as a social value. Up to now we have been concerned mainly with the traditional function of the school as an agent of socialization and social control, albeit in a society characterized by rapid change. However, as a society we have decreed that the responsibility of our schools shall not end with the maintenance of the status quo nor even with the socialization of individuals who are able to adapt easily to a changing social and physical environment, but instead shall extend to the maximum encouragement of the creative abilities of new members of the society. Thus, paradoxically, educational institutions have assumed a major role as agents of innovation and change along with their conservative role in assuring the cultural continuity of the society.

These conflicting views of the school's function in the society have created very real problems for educational institutions at all levels. Current debates over what should be the relative emphasis on the classics as opposed to the sciences, the social sciences, and the creative arts may be viewed as a part of this broader issue. Similarly, questions of the degree to which children should be free to question the wisdom (and authority) of their elders (including their teachers), the extent to which the learning process should be based primarily on rote memorization of basic facts and principles, and even whether going to school should be viewed as "fun" or hard work, bear a direct relationship to the part one believes the school should play in society. The conflict also can be seen clearly in criticisms of the scholarly dictum of "publish or perish" and the growing volume of financial and other rewards for the researcher that have resulted in a shortage of good teachers in our universities and colleges.

The attribution to the paradox between the school's conservative and innovative functions of responsibility for all or most of the current educational ferment is perhaps to oversimplify the issues involved. But just as a major part of the great political debate in American society at present can be resolved into a clash between conservative and innovative forces, so can the roots of many educational issues be traced to similar practical and ideological issues. Responsive as they must be to the needs and desires of the society they serve, educational institutions reflect society's indecisions and paradoxes. Unfortunately, while the characterization of educational issues in terms of absolute alternatives helps us to understand more clearly the pressures with which we must deal, it does not provide much in the way of conceptual tools for solving our problems. It is hoped that by attempting to consider in a more or less systematic way the relationships between various functions of the school; the formal and informal mechanisms by which influence is brought to bear on administrators, teachers, parents, and students; and the pressing educational problems of our time, it will be possible to arrive at some useful suggestions for attacking these problems.

THE ROLE OF EDUCATIONAL INSTITUTIONS IN PRODUCING CHANGE

In American society change and "progress" have come to be accepted as major social values. We are not always clear about what we mean by the term progress, but among other things, at least, it refers to technological innovation that results in a reduction in the amount of physical labor necessary for the provision of essential goods and services as well as an increase in the convenience and comfort of our daily lives. Progress also implies a continued increase in our standard of living (however measured), and it may or may not refer to the enrichment and development of our aesthetic heritage.

In a society committed to an ideal of continual change, where successful maintenance of the status quo is more often than not looked upon as tantamount to failure, the role of educational institutions becomes extremely complex. At certain levels in universities and colleges, educational institutions have been given a fairly clear mandate to contribute actively to the change process. Although universities are being chastised for neglecting the teaching function, the importance and legitimacy of the part played by the university scholar in the discovery of new knowledge has never been questioned. The greatest amount of ambivalence about the proper activities of educational institutions in regard to stimulating change is encountered at the elementary and secondary school level. The mandate of the school to inculcate basic intellectual skills along with a fixed cultural heritage contrasts most sharply here with its responsibility to help children to cope successfully with a society that in many respects may be dramatically different from the one that exists at present or the one that their parents and teachers grew up in. The question facing educators and parents alike is what skills and knowledge our children will have to have in order to make the adjustment to tomorrow's adult society and further, to be able to contribute intelligently to the continued development of the society. It is over this question that much of the battle between educational conservatives and progressives rages, although the real issue is often obscured by clouds of emotional steam generated by the participants.

Few educators or parents would seriously quarrel with the statement that the ultimate aim of the school is to prepare children to participate intelligently and productively as adult members of our society by providing them with the knowledge, skills, and habits they will need for this purpose. It is disagreement over the *means* one ought to use to achieve this goal and, even more important, disagreement over the *particular kinds of abilities and knowledge* our children will need if they are to be able to function effectively as adults. At stake are educational techniques as well as decisions about immediate and specific educational goals. Max Rafferty presents the conservative point of view in his statement that "only through a program of basic education that stresses the importance of offering and mastering organized, systematic, and disciplined subject matter do boys and girls learn the really important things. Familiarity with our cultural heritage does *not* arise spontaneously and inevitably out of the permissive, Pollyanna-ish 'life-adjustment' approach to instruction. Contrary to what the progressive educationists would have us believe, a child will *not* necessarily learn the location of Nyasaland by building a mud hut in the middle of the classroom floor, any more than he will understand the historical importance of the North American Indian migrations by making a Hopi Kachina mask out of papier-maché."[1] Although the issues here are far from simple, Rafferty comes perilously close to asserting that memorization (mastery) of the geographical coordinates of Nyasaland (organized, systematic, and disciplined subject matter) is of greater importance than the acquisition at some deeper (and presumably less disciplined) level of an understanding of the culture of the people of Nyasaland.

The ability to innovate, to create a new art form or a new machine, or to produce a new solution to new problems in international affairs unquestionably requires a mastery of subject matter as well as a degree of intellectual discipline. But it also depends on a capacity for flexibility and the willingness to discard traditional techniques for approaching a problem, particularly when the problems one is interested in solving are themselves changing rapidly and continually, not only in superficial content but also in their formal structure. Assuming that our society and others throughout the world will continue to change at their current rates during the coming decades, we would argue that our present educational system must do more than provide students with a "mastery of organized, systematic, and disciplined subject matter" if they are to be able to react in appropriate ways to the unique situations they will face as policy-makers and citizens of a world community in the twenty-first century. In fact, it appears likely that unless we take some major steps toward gearing our educational system to produce large numbers of highly sophisticated and flexible problem solvers in the immediate future, we may not reach the twenty-first century, either as individuals or as a society.

The difficulty is that our capacity as a society for technological innovation has outstripped our ability to produce the *social* innovations necessary to accommodate either our changing technology or the changes wrought by our advancing technical skills. We are in a situation where we know a great deal more about prolonging life from a physiological standpoint than we do about how to make life productive and interesting for our elder citizens. We have made great strides in the development of computers with enormous capacities for facilitating decision-making processes by simultaneously considering many more variables than any individual or group of individuals, but we still know comparatively little about how decisions actually are made in many of the critical policy-making bodies of our society. We have created devices that make it possible for individual human beings literally to destroy civilization as we know it without creating at the same time any viable way of managing our political relationships with other societies or even of effectively controlling the use of the devices we have created that threaten our own existence.

How has such a situation arisen? Apparently our present educational system has produced a sufficient number of highly creative individuals to have solved many extraordinarily complex scientific and technical problems. Either this innovative talent has not been focused on resolving our interpersonal and intergroup problems or the difficulties we face in the social sphere are of a different order of magnitude (or perhaps a different form altogether) from those with which we have had so much success in the physical sciences. Probably the answer lies in both areas. One major difference between problems in the physical and social sciences is that in chemistry or physics it is much easier to track one's experimental variables into a corner for study than it is in psychology, sociology, economics, or political science. In addition, for a number of reasons we have tended to focus our interest as a society primarily on the accomplishments of the physical and natural sciences, with the result that other fields have received a disproportionately smaller share of our resources, both material and intellectual.

Perhaps the most important factor in the lag between our accommodation to the physical world and our control over the social environment, however, is the fact that the management of interpersonal and intergroup relations requires a minimum degree of competence on the part of *all* of the participants. Public affairs, on both the national and international level as well as in the local community, depend to a very great extent on the capabilities and sophistication of each and every citizen, especially in a democratic society. All of this implies that it is not enough for our schools to turn out a small number of intellectually sophisticated and creative individuals while contenting themselves with making sure that the bulk of the population can read a newspaper, figure out their income tax, and tell their children who George Washington was. Granting the limitations on the distribution of intellectual abilities in the population as a whole, it would appear to be imperative for all who bear a responsibility for education in the country, from government officials to parents, to alter their conception of the aims of the educational system dramatically. Schools must prepare all members of the society to cope effectively with their environment, both physical *and* social, and to provide them with the skills necessary to participate with other citizens in solving the complex and rapidly changing problems facing their communities, their nation, and their world. It is the contention of this writer that this can only be accomplished by an educational system that aims for more than subject matter competence, not only for the most intelligent and gifted children but for the bulk of our population as well.

Faced with an increasing gap between our technical skills and our inability to solve the social problems created by these capabilities, one's awareness of the importance of the innovative function of our educational institutions and their particular responsibility vis-à-vis the creation of a citizenry that is capable of closing this gap is overwhelming. But an awareness of the educational problems our society faces does not automatically provide us with the solution to these problems. It would appear that existing educational techniques—be they traditional or "progressive"—will require substantial modification if we are to make the most of our human resources. Thus far it is not clear in what direction we should be moving. Unfortunately we know very little at the present time about what kinds of educational experiences result in the desired combination of intellectual flexibility and content mastery. Nevertheless a number of the issues that have been raised concerning educational policy may be considered in the light of the above argument, and some speculations may be advanced about where answers to these questions may be found. The remainder of this chapter will be devoted to a consideration of some of these points as well as to a more detailed analysis of the ways in which educational institutions in the United States contribute to the process of social change.

INNOVATION AND CURRICULUM CONTENT

A major point of controversy in educational policy discussions at present concerns the extent to which elementary and secondary school curricula ought to include subject matter that is peripheral to what is usually considered to be the traditional core of educational concern: reading, writing, arithmetic, science, history, geography, foreign languages (including classical languages), and civics. The debate usually centers on the value of including instruction in art, music, social studies (particularly where this means studying the culture of other societies in contrast to geography and history), cooking, sewing, hygiene, many vocational subjects, and a variety of other courses with even less academic titles.[2] The controversy also involves teaching methods: should children be taught by the traditional techniques of reading, memorization, and class recitation or, on the other hand, by providing them with as wide a variety of learning experiences as possible (for example, the "mud hut" on the classroom floor), or by some combination of these approaches.

At the outset it should be made clear that the traditional subjects and methods are no less relevant today than they were fifty or a hundred years ago. As the number of unskilled jobs decreases and the proportion of white collar and highly skilled blue collar positions in the labor force increases, the importance of a firm grounding in basic intellectual skills grows accordingly. And although we have a long way to go in attaining a uniformly high level of educational accomplishment in the society, the available evidence indicates a steadily upward trend over the last half century.

On the other hand, we would not agree with those who would do away with art, music, or social studies in our schools, or those who would reject out-of-hand pedagogical innovations that aim at increasing a child's reasoning power at the expense of practice in memorization, whether of multiplication tables or Chaucer and Shakespeare. As the pace of change in our society and the rest of the world accelerates, increasingly we are going to face intellectual challenges that will not yield to solution by rote application of old techniques. These challenges will require the development of new problem-solving techniques that are unlikely either to be produced, appreciated, or applied by minds that have been shackled into a deductive mold by an educational experience that is based entirely or primarily on memorization and recitation. Likewise, the complexity of the problems we are encountering in the management of our affairs both at home and abroad demands a citizenry that is sensitive to differences between our culture and the cultures of the many peoples with whom we must deal, including different groups within our own society. If the acquisition of this kind of sensitivity requires mud huts in classrooms, excursions to museums, or visits to ethnic enclaves within our cities, then we must be prepared to provide our children with this kind of learning experience even though its effect may be difficult to measure in objective terms.

This does not necessarily mean that education should be easy or "soft" in conservative terms. There seems to be no reason why *interesting* and *difficult* must be viewed as mutually exclusive characteristics of subject matter or why departures from the old standby techniques of memorization and recitation automatically imply that teachers are "pampering" students. It is quite possible to conceive of elementary and secondary school courses in which a considerable degree of intellectual rigor and sophistication is demanded of students within a pedagogical framework that allows the student to approach the problem in his own way and to make use of a variety of sources of information in obtaining a solution. Critical factors, of course, in the success of such courses are the student's familiarity with basic intellectual skills, such as reading and writing, and the level of accomplishment that is demanded by the teacher (which in turn is dependent on the teacher's own level of sophistication). The problem may be rephrased as one of achieving a balance between providing the student with the intellectual tools he must have in order to function in today's changing society and giving him an opportunity to make use of those skills in novel ways in problem situations characterized by some degree of sophistication and complexity.

From this point of view the inclusion of social studies, art, music, and other courses that deepen the intellectual sophistication of students are not only appropriate but indispensable as long as they are not offered as substitutes for more basic subjects and providing that they are taught on a level and in a manner that challenges children to make the fullest use of their skills.

The present argument is based on the assumption that a direct relationship exists between responses a child learns to make to his educational environment and the way he will respond to the various intellectual and social problems that will confront him as an adult. As has been pointed out above, children acquire not only subject matter competence in school but also a variety of problem-solving skills. These skills aid them in solving business problems, figuring out their income taxes, deciding who or what to vote for, acquiring new and specialized skills on their jobs, and working out family disagreements. The particular techniques involved vary from procedures for doing long division to predispositions about how one evaluates a candidate for political office or adjudicates among incompatible demands from one's children.

Clearly, total responsibility for the way adults handle the multitude of problems with which they must deal on a daily basis cannot be attributed to our educational institutions. We have already noted the important role of family and peer group in the socialization process. Nor does this process, including the acquisition of new problem-solving techniques and skills, end with the termination of formal schooling or with establishment of one's own family. Socialization and resocialization can, and does, occur continually as the individual moves from group to group and from stage to stage in his life cycle. Nevertheless the school remains the focal point in this process during the critical early years, and the influence of the individual's formal educational experiences on his later life adjustment to society is likely to be an enduring one.

Two major reasons may be advanced for the primacy of educational influences. In the first place the society legitimizes the importance of the school by its increasing concern for education. In recent years education has come to be viewed by many members of the society as the key to the solution of most of our present ills; consequently, a greater and greater share of the society's resources have been allocated to educational enterprises. At the same time, as the society has become more technologically complex, education has become increasingly specialized and professionalized. The result has been a widening gap between the parent and the teacher in respect to presumed if not actual technical expertise, and a transference of more and more of the responsibility for at least the formal educational aspects of socialization from the family to the school. Teachers have grown in professional status and influence as their job has grown in complexity, and the importance of the skills they are responsible for passing on to their students has increased.

Secondly, formal educational institutions have their impact at a period in the life cycle during which the major focus of the child's activities is on the acquisition of strategies for dealing with the world around him. When the child enters school he must face for the first time in a meaningful context the problem of winning the respect of an elder, his teacher. The child must make the transition from a social system in which the characteristics of one's role in relation to the other members of the group are for the most part *ascribed* or automatically acquired by virtue of one's position in the group (e.g., the family) to a system in which the individual member must *achieve* status in relation to the other individuals in the group. To be sure, achievement in part characterizes role relationships in preschool peer groups, but there is little comparison between peer group and school activities in terms of the relative importance attached to the child's performance by his family and other significant reference figures, and the child knows it. Thus the kinds of things the child must do to maintain his status in the classroom and the techniques he learns from his teachers for handling the intellectual tasks that are part of the work of school are likely to result in relatively stable ways of responding to similar situations in the future. All of the evidence available from studies of attempts to alter behavior patterns that are established during childhood (from psychoanalytic researches, efforts to reform delinquent adolescents, and the like) indicates how powerful these response sets may be.

The conclusion which may be drawn from the preceding observations is that considerably more attention needs to be given to the effect that current pedagogical practices are having on the way children and adults approach and attempt to solve problems. Traditional educational philosophies and methods have tended to be relatively narrow in their approach to subject matter, especially at the elementary level. Most of the presently accepted techniques for teaching children to read, write, and do simple mathematics in the primary grades are based in large part on the principles of deductive logic; that is, the student is taught to apply a previously learned formula or set of propositions and by manipulating the facts and formulas in accordance with appropriate transformation rules arrives at a solution. In learning to multiply, for example, children are first taught a set of rules and then given specific problems on which to practice applying these procedures. In learning to read and write, children are expected to follow the general procedures used by the teacher and the measure of their success is their ability to copy his actions exactly. Obviously, methods requiring children to employ other forms of logic in working out solutions to problems are often used. Nor may any reasoning processes profitably be described wholly in terms of a single system of logic. Nevertheless, the single most important intellectual demand that is made on most children in school is to follow their teacher's example, often regardless of the appropriateness of that example.

Most problems, whether they be concerned with reading or arithmetic, may be approached in a number of different ways. But current educational techniques that orient children to their teachers instead of to the subject matter make it difficult for the child to work out solutions to problems in a way that is different from that of his teacher. If, for whatever reason, the technique for solving the problem offered by the teacher turns out to be incompatible with the peculiar intellectual capacities and propensities of the child, the learning process may be seriously impeded. Similarly, once the child has mastered his teacher's formulas and procedures and has practiced using them over a period of time, he is likely to find it increasingly difficult to alter the way in which he goes about solving a problem—even though the procedure may be inefficient or even inappropriate for the problems he encounters.

To the extent that the cumulative impact of our educational system is to produce individuals who are only able to deal with problems of a certain type (incidentally, it should be made clear that no systematic data exist to substantiate such a hypothesis) major difficulties may be created in a society that requires a high degree of intellectual flexibility from its members as a consequence of rapid change. Previously learned solutions are appropriate only so long as the formulas remain applicable and the basic nature of the problems to be solved remains unchanged. Without the ability to recognize the changing characteristics of situations and the capacity to generate new techniques for handling them, we must continue to make mistakes of the same general order as the child who is unable to comprehend the logic of binary mathematics because of prior rote assimilation of techniques appropriate to the decimal system.

Innovation requires the ability to view one's problem in a new light, to discard inappropriate techniques for solving it, and to work backwards from the observation of reality and the goals one desires to achieve to the derivation of a new principal or technique that makes a new solution possible. Thus far our educational system has done extraordinarily well in producing and encouraging a sufficiently large number of individuals who possess the required innovative skills in scientific and related technical areas to advance the technological capacities of the society at an astonishing rate. It has done less well in generating a citizenry that has the capacity either collectively or individually to adapt easily and in maximally appropriate ways to changes that have resulted from the innovations produced by the scientific community. A premise of this book is that if we are to reduce the gap between our technical accomplishments and the sophistication of our social adaptations to them, our educational system needs a major overhaul—and it needs it badly.

One example of an innovation in teaching methods that places a relatively greater emphasis on inductive as against deductive processes is provided by Omar K. Moore in his work with preschool, kindergarten, and first grade children in the teaching of reading (and more recently foreign languages and mathematics). Moore's technique is based on the creation of a learning environment that is structured in such a way that the learner is "likely to make a series of interconnected discoveries about the physical, cultural or social world"[3] and at the same time (the environment) is responsive to the unique cognitive demands of the individual. "Autotelic responsive environments," as Moore calls such situations, have the following specific characteristics: they permit the learner to explore freely and to try out alternative solutions to the problems presented as long as he abides by a set of basic ground rules; they inform the learner immediately about the consequences of his actions; they are self-pacing, i.e., events happen within the environment at a rate determined by the learner; they permit the learner to make full use of his capacity for discovering relations of various kinds; and finally, they are entered into for their own sake rather than to obtain rewards or avoid punishments that have *no inherent* connection with the activity itself.[4] It can be seen that such a situation has many of the characteristics of inductive logic. Moore has theorized that it is under these conditions that optimal rates of progress in acquiring complex intellectual skills may be achieved.

To demonstrate the effectiveness of autotelic responsive environments as teaching devices, Moore has developed a laboratory built around a computerized "talking typewriter" which teaches children to read by responding in a relatively complex manner to the actions of its user. In Moore's laboratory preschool children are given an opportunity to "play" with these typewriters without any interference (or prodding) from adults. In so doing they acquire basic linguistic skills such as reading, writing, listening, and speaking in a remarkably short time. The key to the effectiveness of the situation is that although the child has considerable freedom to experiment with alternative behaviors and thereby discover the optimum solution to the problems presented in his own way, he must always act within a relatively structured environment—the game has very definite rules (which, however, the child must figure out for himself like everything else). And like most games the situation is *fun*.

In the initial sessions at the typewriter the child may strike any of the keys on the typewriter in any order and with any frequency; he is free to explore the keyboard in his own way. As he strikes each key the typewriter responds immediately by *saying out loud* (via a tape recording) the name of the letter or symbol that has been printed. The child soon realizes that he has a great deal of control over this machine in front of him. If he wants the typewriter to say "a" then all he has to do is strike the key marked *a*. As the child progresses the rules of the game are changed to keep him interested and learning. After the initial period of free exploration of the keyboard, the typewriter takes the initiative in setting more difficult problems for the child to solve. First letters and then words appear on a screen above the carriage and the child soon discovers that the only way he can get the typewriter to work is by striking the key that corresponds to the letter or symbol displayed—all other keys on the keyboard are automatically locked. In each case no one tells the child what to do, he must figure it out for himself, and in the process he rapidly acquires the relevant skills.

In succeeding phases of Moore's procedure children go on to solve a variety of problems, including transcription of dictation (their own), composition of original stories (on the typewriter), and eventually such activities as publishing their own newspaper (including cutting the stencils and running the mimeograph machine). Throughout, the keynote is creating situations that are both inherently interesting to children and that are structured in such a way as to maximize the probability that the child will discover useful relationships and regularities in the symbolic world around him. The children are not just playing with expensive toys in a random manner. They are playing a series of games, the normative structure, content, and sequences of which have been painstakingly created to enable the child to make maximum use of his own inductive and deductive reasoning powers. The relative freedom to explore alternative courses of action, coupled with the lack of serious penalties for errors (for example, parental or teacher disapproval) keeps him from becoming inhibited or frozen into a single way of thinking about the problem, while the normative structure of the situation (the rules of the game) keep him on the learning track.

The results of the work that Moore has done thus far have been highly encouraging. Under these conditions children do learn to read and write in an amazingly short period of time, and they have fun at it. More important, admittedly unsystematic observations indicate that they also develop a high degree of intellectual flexibility and sophistication that is reflected in the content of their stories, their aesthetic activities, and their social and emotional relationships. Although much more work must be done before any overall evaluative judgment can be made on the effectiveness and practicality of Moore's theory and research, the importance of this kind of fresh approach to our educational problems cannot be over-stated. Perhaps the most significant aspect of Moore's work is that it derives out of a consistent conceptualization of the nature of the socialization process viewed in relation to the properties of the society in which we live instead of being, like most educational innovations, an *ad hoc* and piecemeal remedy to a specific educational deficiency.

DISCIPLINE AND PUPIL CREATIVITY

Another important aspect of the controversy between educational progressives and conservatives concerns the question of discipline and authority in the classroom. Wrapped up in this issue are cultural differences in child-rearing patterns and family social structure, the continual conflict between the new generation and the old (which is accentuated in a rapidly changing society), and the problems faced by administrators and teachers who are responsible for providing public education in areas where the response to economic and social frustration has been a rising tide of aggression, mistrust and lack of respect for authority. As a corollary to the questions raised in the preceding section, the problem of the degree to which pupil initiative and freedom should be encouraged in the classroom also bears directly on the larger issue of the relative emphasis that should be placed on the social control as opposed to the innovative functions of educational institutions in our society. Although a number of interesting questions can be raised about the precise nature of the relationship between discipline and creativity (creativity being the subject about which we know less than almost any other in the educational field), a highly authoritarian relationship between teacher and pupil often appears to be associated with a decrement in pupil creativity.

The implicit assumption that an inverse relationship exists between authority and innovation is reflected in Merle Borrowman's statement pointing out the ambivalence that has characterized educational (as well as family) philosophy and practice on this issue:

> The dominant tradition might, then, be characterized as one of continuous tension between an explicit ideal of child submissiveness and implicit delight in the child's asser-

tions of independence from adult authority. Those who have grown up in this tradition will have a certain ambivalence. Perhaps, again, in times when the adult feels that the world, or his own personal life, is "getting out of control," we might expect him to be emotionally offended at the sight of a classroom in which the mantle of authority is lightly worn by adults. Those who feel more secure in their own lives may be expected to be more comfortable in the presence of educational practices which emphasize the initiative and freedom of the child.[5]

Although a clear distinction can be drawn between the exercise of individual initiative and outright defiance of teacher authority involving the disruption of learning processes in the classroom, the line between disobedience and innovative expression becomes more difficult to define as the relationship between teacher and pupil becomes more authoritarian (as defined by the teacher). Thus discipline and the exercise of pupil initiative are not incompatible alternatives so long as demands for obedience do not become so intense that they encompass every aspect of pupil behavior from actions to thoughts.

The important conclusion to be drawn here is the necessity for establishing learning environments that are characterized by clearly defined (and enforced) rules of conduct, but which also are structured in such a way as to permit a maximum amount of pupil exploration, initiative and, hopefully, innovation. This means, among other things, that a distinction must be made within the classroom between *matters of conduct,* the conditions under which the student may express himself and otherwise act, and *matters of intellect,* the way in which the student arrives at a solution to the problem and the kinds of ideas he may hold. In the former case the teacher role demands that he retain and exert the authority to define the student's role; in the latter case his role dictates that he should (1) provide a model for students to emulate, (2) give them the necessary feedback so that they can evaluate the efficacy of their actions, and, (3) encourage innovative approaches and solutions on their part. Tolerance (much less enjoyment) of this kind of a situation by the teacher depends in large part, as Borrowman suggests, on the degree to which the teacher feels secure in his own life and therefore does not perceive pupil creativity and achievement as a threat either to his authority or his ego.

Such an environment depends on the student as well as the teacher. In simplest terms, the pupil must be willing to play the game, to permit the teacher to define his role with respect to matters of conduct and to make use of his assistance in exploring alternative behaviors in regard to matters of intellect. The teacher in the ghetto or the slum school, who must spend all of his time dealing with the accumulated frustration, aggression, and resentment of his pupils, may never have a chance to be concerned with these issues. Consequently his pupils may never have an opportunity to exercise their intellects in a useful way. Granting at least a minimum degree of motivation on the part of children to comply with the authority of the teacher, the role relationship that we are proposing here is almost certainly the one which exists between the well-known "natural teacher" and his pupils, and most principals are fully aware of which teachers in their schools manage to achieve it. It rests on a high degree of teacher respect for his pupils, and vice versa, which is another way of acknowledging the importance of mutual acceptance of the relative roles. Where it is lacking, either because of the inability of the teacher to grant the required degree of intellectual autonomy to his pupils or because of the unwillingness of students to accept his authority in matters of conduct, the school at best struggles to fulfill its function as a transmitter of culture and at worst becomes simply a custodial institution where children are locked up with a teacher for several hours each day to keep them off the street or out of their mother's hair. Under the latter conditions the lack of intellectual stimulation combined with the absence of mutual respect between teacher and students may do much to reinforce the alienation of the child vis-à-vis the school and ultimately perhaps even the society which the school represents.

Creating the proper balance between discipline and the encouragement of pupil innovation is not an easy task, especially when the educational process is complicated by social factors that create rebellion, alienation, and anomie on the part of students. The answer does not lie in permitting students to behave as they please or to study only what they want to study any more than it does in requiring them to think in a certain way or to solve problems in a particular manner. The essential requirements are a sufficient degree of motivation on the part of students to play the game according to its rules, a clear perception on the part of both students and teacher of their respective roles and statuses, and a willingness on the part of the teacher to permit pupils to approach a problem in their own way or to express their own ideas even when there is a possibility that a student will come up with a better solution than his own. It is the teacher's responsibility to establish the ground rules and to set the task; it is the student's responsibility to abide by the rules and to work on the problems set by the teacher. Under these conditions alone may we achieve both discipline and innovation.

A professorial appointment at a college or university traditionally carries with it the obligation on the part of the incumbent to engage in scholarly pursuits, including contributing to the advancement of knowledge through original research and writing, in addition to instructing students. Although there has never been any disagreement over the stipulation that faculty members should have this dual responsibility to be both innovators and transmitters of culture, establishing a proper balance between the two functions has become a major point of contention in academic circles.[6]

Due in large part to a growing volume of public and private support for research activities and to the increased competition for scientific and technical manpower that has been created by this support, the mark of a successful academician has come to be his ability to achieve complete freedom from teaching responsibilities (particularly with regard to undergraduate students) through research grants and other sources of financial support independent of his salary as a member of a college faculty. College and universities, eager for both public recognition and government funds for research facilities, have contributed to the downgrading of the teaching function by enforcing the "publish or perish" dictum, competing with one another in offering reduced teaching loads as an incentive to attract promising scholars to their campuses and encouraging the practice of depending on graduate-student teaching assistants to handle a larger and larger share of the undergraduate teaching load. As a consequence, the balance between undergraduate teaching and research has been tipped significantly in the direction of research and graduate education, much to the distress of many educators who feel that in so doing institutions of higher learning have badly neglected a major function, that of preparing the next generation of scholars and intelligent citizens for positions of leadership and responsibility.

Although this issue directly involves institutions of higher learning, its ramifications are being felt more and more at the secondary school level. As the quality of teaching, and consequently the level of performance that is demanded of undergraduates in many universities and colleges, declines, differences between secondary school curricula and courses offered at the college level tend to be reduced. The once distinct line of demarcation between high school and college has become blurred for many students, particularly those who graduate from the better secondary schools. Instead of offering qualitatively different educational challenges and experiences, college now appears to be more of the same, albeit perhaps a little harder. As universities have turned their attention to graduate training at the expense of undergraduate teaching, the student must now wait for graduate school to experience the change in relationship between teacher and student that formerly accompanied the transition from high school to college.

The tendency for college to become like high school and vice versa is accentuated by changes that are taking place in the structure of our educational system on both sides of the fence between secondary school and college. On the one hand, strong pressures from a variety of sources have resulted in attempts to upgrade elementary and secondary school curricula and in particular to give gifted students an opportunity to move ahead at a faster pace even if this means making what traditionally has been college level material available to them. As a result of these changes, high school teachers, feeling the increased scholarly demands, have taken on many of the characteristics and activities of college faculty members, including advanced degrees and an interest in doing productive work of their own. A growing number of high school teachers have been attending summer institutes and seminars designed to acquaint them with what is going on in their fields, thus increasing their kinship with the college professor who is supposed to keep up with the newest developments in his specialty and accentuating their relationship to the innovative side of the educational process.

On the other hand, the growth and development of the junior college has served to reduce the psychological and pedagogical distance between secondary and higher education. In California over seventy junior colleges scattered throughout the state are required to admit any high school graduate on a tuition-free basis. At the end of two years the successful student may transfer to a four-year state college or to one of the university campuses and receive full credit for the courses taken in the junior college. Is this an extension of high school or a special class of college? It is both, and the school suffers from a number of problems resulting from its indeterminate status.[7] The typical junior college faculty member is aware of the fact that he is of the world of higher education but not really part of it since his heavy teaching responsibilities and lack of research facilities (including graduate student assistants) make original scholarship difficult. In this respect and in regard to the kind of students he must teach, the junior college faculty member is more like the high school teacher than the college professor. In addition, the student tends to perceive the junior college as another barrier to be surmounted in order to get into a "real" college even though he is getting college credit for the work he is doing.

Between the upgrading of the high school curriculum and the introduction of the junior college as a way of relieving the pressure for admission to college (as well as keeping the door to higher education open to students who, for one reason or another, fail to perform well enough in high school to meet higher college entrance standards), the once clear intellectual line between high school and college is being erased. As this process continues we may predict a further sifting down of the innovative functions of the university to the high school and, at the very least, an increasing specialization of interest and concern on the part of high school teachers with developments that are occurring on the growing edge of their fields. Thus it would seem likely that the preoccupation of universities and colleges with graduate education and research will lead to increased concern with the innovative functions of educational institutions at all levels and a blurring of status distinctions between all of those who are responsible for teaching, whether it be at the high school level, the junior college, or the university.

CULTURAL DIVERSITY AND SOCIAL CHANGE

During the past two decades significant changes in both organizational characteristics and programs have done much to shift the focus of the school away from a primary concern with maintaining the status quo toward an acceptance of the special responsibilities of educational institutions in a changing society. In a number of different ways the orientation of the school has been changed and broadened. The once predominant preoccupation with the affairs and cultural traditions of the local community has diminished, and the school, like the nation itself, has become involved in the problems of the broader society, its cultural contrasts and conflicts, and its relations with the rest of the world. The face of the school has been turned toward the future as well as toward the world beyond our shores, and for the first time in our short history a determined assault is being made on the fortresses of ethnocentrism, isolationism, and unyielding traditionalism, both at the community and national level. The sources of these shifts in educational interest are varied and certainly include such influences as the continuing developments in communication and transportation, our involvement in the Second World War, the struggle between communism and capitalism, and the recent imagination-capturing advances into space. In addition to these external influences, a major factor in this process has been the growing cultural diversity that has characterized our schools; a diversity which has been fostered and encouraged by several important changes in the structure and nature of our educational institutions.

THE INCREASING HETEROGENEITY OF SCHOOL POPULATIONS

Perhaps the most important structural change that has taken place in American education has been the increasing centralization of school districts and the gradual disappearance of not only the one room school, but the small town school as well. In rural and other small communities their place has been taken by the consolidated school serving a much larger area and to which pupils travel by bus. Similarly, in urban areas the major developments have been the increased size of individual schools within school districts, particularly at the secondary level, and the appearance of special purpose schools, such as vocational schools and schools for the gifted and the retarded, that crosscut the traditional neighborhood pattern. These changes in organization have come about as a result of a variety of influences, including population growth, the desire for economies in basic costs—from physical plants to the most efficient use of teachers—that are possible with consolidation, demands for more highly specialized educational services that are only feasible with a larger pupil body (for example, extensive school libraries, remedial reading, science and language laboratories, training in music and the arts, physical educational facilities), and the greatly increased mobility on the part of the population due to advances in transportation technology and the general standard of living.

The effect of these organizational changes has been in general to increase substantially both the size and heterogeneity of the student populations of schools with respect to social class variation as well as religious, racial, and ethnic composition. Under these conditions schools as well as pupils and teachers have been forced to acknowledge the existence of social and cultural differences and to work out not only ways of accommodating these differences, but techniques for taking advantage of the educational opportunities they provide as well. Classroom programs in which children have an opportunity to learn about one another's religious beliefs or unique cultural traditions provide examples of ways schools have used the heterogeneity of their student body to advantage. In addition to helping penetrate personal barriers of ethnocentrism and prejudice, it is apparent that the increasing cultural diversity of our schools has served to encourage (as well as facilitate) the introduction of curriculum materials designed explicitly to broaden the perspective from which children view their society and the world. The increased size of schools, and consequently of faculties, has also made possible the addition of teachers having a wider range of interests, backgrounds, and professional competencies than heretofore feasible.

Evidence that schools are indeed broadening their perspectives as well as their curricula may be seen everywhere, from the increasing market for social studies textbooks to the growing number of student exchange programs designed explicitly to increase the heterogeneity of the student body (as well as the sophistication of participating students). Since it is inconceivable that cultural contact, whether through books or personal experience, can take place without some degree of modification or adaptation on the part of both parties, the school is contributing materially to the process of social change and innovation through its orientation toward different cultures.

Recent pressures for school integration and the elimination of *de facto* racial segregation through modifications in the pattern of neighborhood schools have added to the rate at which schools, particularly those in urban areas, are becoming relatively heterogeneous in character. The controversy over segregated schooling serves to emphasize the importance of culture contact in the process of social change. Rights spokesmen point out that merely providing the Negro with educational advantages equal to those of white children is not enough. They recognize that Negroes must have an opportunity to associate with members of the dominant middle-class white society if they are ever to be able to participate on an equal basis in an integrated society. Although perhaps overestimating the extent to which a few hours a day of such contact can produce noticeable changes in the culture of Negro children so long as the majority of their significant relationships and experiences take place in the ghetto, Negro leaders press their demands with a clear understanding of many of the basic processes involved in social change.

THE ROLE OF THE MASS MEDIA

The tremendous growth of the mass media during the last ten years has contributed in large measure to the increasing diversity of the experiences to which children are exposed, both in school and out. Paradoxically, it has added also to the tendency toward the creation of a mass culture. Thus the impact of the mass media on the school has been both to make possible a richer and more varied educational experience and to speed up the process of acculturation and the consequent disappearance of distinct cultural traditions within segments of the society. Television in particular has a very great effect on the school and on the children who come to school to be taught. As Wilbur Schramm put it:

> There is no doubt, of course, that television is contributing to the cognitive and evaluative resources of the young

child. By the age of 3, over 30 per cent of children in the United States are already making regular use of television, calling for their favorite programs and imitating their picture-tube heroes. By kindergarten age, 80 per cent of children are regular users of television; by first grade, 90 per cent. Throughout elementary school, the average use of television climbs slowly from a little over two hours to a little over three hours a day. A considerable percentage of children consistently average four hours or more a day. This is an enormous commitment of time and it is accompanied by interest and attention at a very high level. It is unbelievable that such a commitment would not make some changes in the kind of child who comes to school to be educated.[8]

Schramm goes on to indicate, however, that current studies do not show children to be very different as a consequence of their extensive exposure to television. Television sends children into the first grade with larger vocabularies (an advantage which appears to be dissipated within a few years, due, perhaps, to the redundancy of the medium as well as to the failure of the school to make the most of its head start), a large excess of fantasy images over reality images, and a sophistication about such things as Santa Claus, boy-girl relations, and the like, which throws the traditional educational timetable considerably askew.

In coping with, or taking advantage of (depending on how one looks at the situation), the impact of television, Schramm suggests that schools will have to learn to compete on the basis of the excitement of learning (a task that will not be easy considering the virtually total commitment of television to excitement) and, on the other hand, attempt to influence viewing habits by making use of television as a basis for assignments—for example, cultural programs, press conferences, political conventions, and the like. Used properly, television may contribute in significant ways to the deepening and enrichment of the cultural experiences of children. Precisely the opposite result may occur, however, if sufficient effort is not devoted to making sure that children spend their television-watching time in maximally productive ways. This is another area in which parent-teacher cooperation is of critical importance. If the mass media are not to circumvent many promising achievements within the educational field, both educators and informed citizens must turn their attention to developing ways of facilitating their cooperation.

Within the school instructional television offers a great many opportunities for supplementing the curriculum and providing highly specialized or rare educational experiences, but it also carries with it some of the risks that attend the misuse of any pedagogical technique. Television is no substitute for direct teacher-student contact, and although it does enable the exceptional teacher to reach a larger number of students, school personnel must be constantly aware of the special demands that are made on both the television teacher and the classroom teacher when this technique is used. Not only is special preparation necessary on the part of the instructional staff, but research has indicated that a critical factor in the success of television teaching is student motivation, a variable that is likely to be much more difficult to control when the teaching is being done on television.

We may conclude that the overall contribution of television to the educational process thus far has been in the direction of increasing the potential diversity of experiences available to children and thereby supporting the role of the school in facilitating the process of social change. Whether we shall capitalize on the opportunities offered by television to further enrich the educational process or whether we shall continue to permit it to have a homogenizing effect on our culture and on the minds of our children remains to be seen.

CHAPTER SIX

•

The Development

and

Allocation of Manpower

•

All societies must train their members to perform the tasks necessary for the continuation and development of the society. In addition they must provide for the allocation of individuals to positions in the society. The importance of these two functions is reflected in the fact that, to the best of our knowledge, no society leaves the development and allocation of manpower to chance, although a great variety of means have been, and are, used to accomplish these ends. In general, the techniques by which individuals are channeled into one position or another (and frequently given opportunities for one kind of training as opposed to another) may be classified into those that are based largely on ascribed (or inherent) characteristics of the individual and those that are based on the individual's achievements or performance. In primitive societies, and to a lesser but still significant extent in our own society, an ascribed characteristic on which many important distinctions are made is sex, women immediately being eliminated as candidates for many positions in the society (the same holds true, of course, for men). Similarly, race, age, birth order, ethnic group membership, and family background all are likely to play a more or less important part in the process of status ascription in modern as well as primitive societies.

Since the adequate performance of most adult roles requires considerable training, particularly in technologically advanced societies, Ralph Linton postulated that the earlier an individual's training for a position begins, the more successful and complete it is likely to be, and consequently the more able the individual will be to perform his duties. The validity of Linton's observations can be seen in the fact that, historically, allocation to positions in the society has more often than not preceded the acquisition of the requisite skills, as in the case of the apprenticeship system and, in advanced societies, selective admission to college. The intimate relationship between the development of well-trained manpower and the most efficacious allocation of that manpower is made more salient as the society becomes more technologically complex and both the skills necessary and the period of training involved in the successful performance of many roles are multiplied.

These changes in the manpower needs of the society and the resulting convergence of allocation and training functions have substantially increased the role of the school in this process for two fairly obvious reasons. In the first place, demands are being made on educational institutions to produce individuals having a greater and greater variety of specialized skills, from the capacity to operate a linotype machine to the techniques involved in programming a computer or designing a bridge. The appearance of the vocational high school and increasing specialization (with concomitant emphasis on technical and professional fields) at the college and university level provide evidence of the growing pressure of society's manpower needs and the reflection of these needs in educational policy and practice. These changes serve to underscore the tendency of educational institutions to speed up the inculcation of practical skills at the expense of those fields having less apparent and immediate relevance to the needs of the society. In addition, the ascendency of a technical, specialized and, above all, practical curriculum in our schools and colleges has had the effect of increasing the degree to which an individual's academic performance may be used to predict his subsequent occupational performance (although there are still many problems in making such predictions on the basis of academic performance), thereby enhancing the role of the school in the allocation process.

Secondly, the cost, degree of specialization, and length of the training period necessary for an increasing proportion of the positions in society makes it impractical either from a societal or an individual standpoint to put all of the members of the society through every possible kind of training, or even to give everyone an extensive opportunity to try out for any occupational specialty they desire. The waste of already scarce and overworked instructional manpower that would result if we were to give anybody who wanted it a year in medical school would be enormous. Not only do individuals differ significantly in their ability to benefit from various kinds of educational experiences, but in addition, the society must ensure a sufficient supply of trained manpower to fill each of the diverse positions necessary to its smooth functioning. Consequently, some means of differentiating among potential candidates for medical school, college, vocational school, and an unlimited number of other more or less specialized educational opportunities is necessary. In addition to serving as a manpower proving and training ground, therefore, the school also fulfills an important function in screening individuals according to their abilities and occupational inclinations at various stages in their intellectual and physical development. Thus allocation takes place prior to entrance to many educational institutions as well as during the course of training and subsequent to it on the basis of one's performance.

As a consequence of their role in the development and allocation of manpower, educational institutions have been forced to take on a number of additional activities—for example, systematic and regular pupil evaluation, the provision of counseling and guidance services, and, frequently, highly bureaucratized admissions offices. They have also become involved in a number of related issues, the solutions to which are of critical importance if our educational institutions are to have any hope of fulfilling their functions in the most efficacious way. For example, in addition to being asked to participate in the development of the most efficient means for the identification of talent, the evaluation of pupil performance, and the prediction of postacademic success, schools have also been given a share of the responsibility for making maximum use of the talent available. This involves considerations of what to do with individuals whose skills have become outmoded by changes in the technology of the society, how to take advantage of the capabilities of women, what to do about that group of individuals whose innate abilities are below the level necessary for adequate performance of a majority of occupational roles, and how to provide maximum opportunities for members of all racial, ethnic, and social class groups to receive an education commensurate with their abilities. The remainder of this chapter will be devoted to ways in which school and college personnel, along with other interested groups in the society, have attempted to solve these problems and to some speculations about how changes in the social and technological structure of the society are likely to affect both the problems and their solutions during the coming decades.

THE IDENTIFICATION OF TALENT

The phrase *identification of talent* implies at the outset that individuals differ in their ability to perform various tasks and that it is possible in some manner to discover which individuals possess which talents. As the phrase is typically used, the implication is that the "talents" referred to are in some measure inherited or at least inborn. Even where there is no assumption of the existence of innate abilities, the reference is usually to selection that precedes long-term performance and specialized training as opposed to that which is based on an evaluation of an individual's performance over time. When we set out to "discover" talent we more often than not are trying to find individuals who give some evidence of having a particular skill or ability, but who may or may not have had an opportunity to develop it to its fullest potential.

Society's demands for skilled manpower and the pressures of a growing (and better educated) population on our educational facilities have made it necessary for schools and colleges to become more and more concerned about the early identification of talent in order to make sure that no able individuals are overlooked and to facilitate the process of allocating scarce educational resources among those who have the greatest capacity to take advantage of them. Fifty years ago the major choice points in a person's educational career were whether he would finish high school and then whether he would go on to college. The latter decision was influenced to a great extent by the ability of one's family to pay for a college education and only incidentally by the unsystematic and relatively subjective selection procedures utilized at that time by the colleges involved. Some few colleges made use of admissions tests of one sort or another, primarily of an essay type, while most schools relied heavily on the applicant's high school record along with an assessment of his family background, character, and the like. Since high schools varied greatly (and still do) in the quality of training they offered students, the better universities and colleges tended to rely heavily on a few private preparatory schools with which they were familiar to provide them with the bulk of their students.

By the late 1940's, however, this picture had changed radically. This was due both to increasing pressure for college admission and to the wide use of objective tests, the development of which was stimulated by the need for better ways of predicting college performance, especially for applicants from high schools of varying quality. As the competition for college admission has grown and the society has, at least in many areas, turned away from such criteria as family background, race, and ethnic origin in allocating educational and occupational opportunities, the search for objective ways to evaluate an individual's abilities and talents has been intensified. The result has been twofold. In the first place, there has been a greater dependence on objective, standardized tests of intelligence, aptitude, and academic achievement (used along with the traditional criterion of school grades) in deciding what kind of educational opportunities an individual will have. A growing volume of scholarship and loan funds has tended to reduce the correlation between family wealth and educational opportunities for advanced education (although this relationship still exists) and the highly able student is finding it more and more difficult to avoid a college education (the student of average or slightly above average intelligence still presents a problem, particularly if. he comes from a lower socioeconomic background).

The other major impact of the recent interest in the identification of talent has been the tendency for schools to attempt to classify children according to their abilities at an earlier age. Around the turn of the century and even as recently as prior to the end of the Second World War, the process of formal classification and evaluation of students' abilities did not begin much before the latter part of high school, except perhaps in the case of the exceptional child or where parents elected to send their children to a private school. Today, however, formal evaluation, including standardized tests and systematic record keeping, begins for most children in elementary school and frequently as early as the first or second grade. In an effort to identify children with exceptional abilities, as well as those who require special help in overcoming deficiencies in prior training or ability, the great majority of school systems make extensive use of both standardized intelligence and achievement tests from the elementary grades through junior high school and high school. In a recent survey of elementary schools' testing programs in New York, Connecticut, and New Jersey,[1] it was discovered that only one school out of more than seven hundred did not use at least one standardized test between kindergarten and grade six. Similar findings have been reported for secondary schools on a nationwide basis.[2]

The widespread use of standardized ability tests from kindergarten to senior high school is a comparatively new development in American education. It reflects the urgency that is felt to make sure no child fails to receive educational opportunities commensurate with his talents. The roots of this sentiment are both utilitarian and equalitarian; utilitarian in the sense that educators and the public alike are aware of the importance of making maximum use of available talent (especially in the light of the current competition with the Soviet Union), and equalitarian in the sense that there is a consciousness of the national ideal of equal opportunity for all. Thus, happily, it is both in the national interest and compatible with the broader values and traditions of the society to encourage the identification and development of talent.

One of the important effects of this filtering down through the educational system of the process of formal evaluation of individual abilities, with its emphasis on the discovery of talent, has been to advance significantly many of the critical choice points in an individual's life. It used to be that what happened to a child in elementary school had very little impact on his chances of getting into college. Most children underwent basically the same kinds of educational experiences through the first eight or nine grades, and although teachers and administrators have no doubt always recognized that some children are more likely to end up in college than others, until recently few decisions having a potential long-range influence were made about a child on the basis of estimates of his abilities prior to the high school years. Today, on the other hand, several decisions of potential educational significance are made about most children long before they reach high school. In the first place, earlier decisions are made about enrollment in subjects that lead either to a college preparatory or a vocational curriculum in secondary school; for example, many elementary and junior high schools are beginning to offer more than token instruction in foreign languages, science, and advanced mathematics. And secondly, more and more schools allocate children to different classes according to their abilities, usually in part on the basis of standardized test scores.

In the previously mentioned elementary school survey, nearly half of the schools reported allocating children to special classes on the basis of ability, and virtually all of the remainder indicated that they group children within classes for instructional purposes. Although most of the evidence concerning the effect of homogeneous grouping on learning, motivation of students, and the like has been inconclusive (as one can imagine, the methodological difficulties in conducting evaluative research of this type are very great), few educators or social scientists would disagree with the statement that homogeneous grouping has advantages insofar as it makes possible a better fit between the needs and capabilities of the student and the characteristics of the curriculum. Thus, for example, given a limit on teacher resources (an almost universal characteristic of school systems) homogeneous grouping may make it possible to allocate these resources more efficiently (the French teacher can concentrate her efforts on only those students who in the long run will benefit most from the study of foreign language).

The theory behind homogeneous grouping is that it benefits both the slower students as well as the brightest by removing the necessity for them to compete against one another and by making it possible for the teacher to set the level of discourse at a point all of the children in the class can understand. If it is assumed that there are any special advantages to be gained from being placed in a class with the most intelligent children in one's grade and given an opportunity to work ahead at a faster pace, the decision to place or not to place a child in such a group may have a long-range impact on both his educational experiences and his life chances. The most severe problems are raised, of course, when one considers the child who is almost qualified for the superior group (or the child who is almost qualified for a normal class instead of one for retarded children). In the borderline case one is on much less firm ground in arguing that the experiences the child will have in the "average" class (or the retarded class) will be better for him than those he would have had in the superior group for which he is almost qualified. The complexity of the situation is illustrated by Daniels' findings in a study done in England that the impact of grouping (or "streaming" as they term it) is primarily to retard the progress of those children in the slower groups (compared to what would have been expected of them had they been in a mixed class) while not adding materially to the progress of those children in the faster groups.[3]

Whatever the effect of grouping on the academic progress of the pupils involved, the experience of being in such a group may have a significant impact on the motivations and aspirations of students, although again we face an absence of any systematic data. Furthermore, from a sociological standpoint it seems fairly clear that any policy or practice which tends to crystallize the social structure of the organization, as does homogeneous grouping, is likely to have additional ramifications for both the organization and the individuals involved. As I have pointed out elsewhere,[4] ability grouping alters the social structure of the school by providing a more clear-cut basis for social differentiation of the student body. Instead of encouraging the less able to come in contact with the gifted in many different activities, ability grouping accentuates natural tendencies for individuals to interact more with others similar to themselves. In the process the gap between children of varying abilities is widened, subcultural differences can be expected to develop, and, to the extent that aptitude is associated with social class, a higher degree of class crystallization may even be anticipated. This pattern will be facilitated not only by the attitudes of children toward one another, but also by changed perceptions of pupils by the school staff.

An important added characteristic of formal evaluation procedures, including standardized testing, is that the results of these measurements more often than not become part of the pupil's permanent record along with his grades and teacher's comments. Although the validity and reliability of all standardized tests is far from perfect, a precise numerical score frequently takes on a kind of absolute validity when it appears on a child's record card. Teachers and administrators alike, when confronted with a child's IQ score or his percentile rank on an achievement test like the Iowa Test of Basic Skills, often tend to disregard the considerable degree of imprecision that is inherent in such measures. Although test publishers and developers have done a conscientious job of trying to educate potential users with regard to the limitations of their products, my observation has been that psychometric sophistication on the part of school personnel tends to be manifested primarily in the abstract or, at best, reserved for special cases where test data are badly out of line with other kinds of information. Thus it may be hypothesized that IQ scores tend to be taken pretty much at face value when decisions must be made about a pupil or when teachers evaluate children's performances.

The conclusion that may be drawn from these observations is that in a variety of ways we are tending to put individuals into cubby holes or, if you will, onto different tracks, at an earlier and earlier age. The implications of these developments for both the child and the school are clear. For example, from the standpoint of the child who has any hopes or expectations of going on to college, it is becoming increasingly important that he do well during the elementary grades, both on standardized tests and in the classroom, in order to maximize his opportunities to receive special instruction, to be placed in an advanced group (if one exists), and to be permitted to enroll in college preparatory courses in junior high school and high school. His test scores are especially important if he wishes to be categorized as potential college material by his teachers, counselor, and principal—both current and future—since his record card will follow him throughout his primary and secondary school experience. Most of his teachers will either be given or have access to the record of his prior performances on standardized intelligence, aptitude, and achievement tests.

From the standpoint of the school in general, the trend appears to be toward a greater degree of social differentiation and structure, although along the lines of ability and achievement, as opposed to the traditional bases of social class, race, or religious group affiliation. Just what these changes will mean in terms of the school's impact on its clients remains to be seen. From the point of view of the future of the testing movement there would seem to be little doubt that the continued pressure to identify able individuals will reinforce and extend current testing practices. We are in for testing with a vengeance, and while the concern for providing maximum

educational opportunities is clearly necessary to the continued progress of the society, we must stay alert to the various possible secondary effects of testing on the educational process and the individuals
involved.

THE MINING APPROACH VS. THE FARMING APPROACH

We have suggested that one of the bases for the concept of
talent identification is belief in the existence of innate differences
in abilities from one individual to another, including the implication
that some individuals may possess more ability (in general) than
others. The best scientific evidence available from the fields of genetics
and developmental psychology indicates that individuals do differ
inherently in their capacity to acquire various skills and in their
ability to perform one task or another, although the precise nature—
for example, to what extent genetically or physiologically determined
—and extent of innate variability in human abilities remains an open
question.

One may draw any one of a number of different conclusions
concerning the implications of these findings for arriving at a solution of society's manpower problems. One may take the position that
manpower development and allocation is essentially a question of discovering which individuals have the innate capacities to perform the
necessary tasks, including learning the requisite skills along the way.
Or one may conclude that the contribution of innate factors to the
resulting total variance in manifest ability is relatively small, and
therefore, while not neglecting the part played by innate ability
entirely, we should concentrate our efforts on making the environment
in which individuals develop their talents more fertile. In the former
case the analogy is to the process involved in discovering, extract-
ing, and refining the mineral resources of the earth—essentially a
mining approach. The latter view is analogous to plant cultivation
in which the strain of seed is important but less so than the ferti-
lizer, soil, irrigation, and sunshine that make up the growing organism's environment. The two points of view are not mutually exclusive in a strict sense: paying close attention to inherent capacity
does not preclude an interest in providing the individual with the
best possible environment in which to learn. In practice, however, the
more genetically oriented approach has the effect of narrowing one's
perception of the limits to which an individual's capacities may be
developed, whereas an emphasis on the contribution of the environment leads to a somewhat more optimistic view of the extent to
which inborn abilities may be manipulated by society.

These points are of both immediate and long-range importance
for the establishment of educational policy. In the short run the

views of the teacher or counselor concerning the degree to which an individual may improve his genetic endowment are likely to have a significant impact on the kinds of advice offered to and decisions made about their pupils or counselees. They will also have much to do with the standards teachers set for their pupils and the kinds of performance demanded of them.

The salutary educational effect of a wide-open view of human intellectual capacity may be seen in a comparison between current Russian educational practice at the elementary school level and our own policies. In the Soviet Union the official point of view on inherent differences in abilities between individuals is that they do not exist except in the case of brain damage or similar physiological causes. Differences in performance are acknowledged, of course, but are attributed solely to motivational factors or to inequalities in prior experience. This fervently held belief in innate equality shifts the focus of educators to the question of how to motivate children to meet the highest possible standards and generates great pressure to raise the overall educational level of the society. In the elementary classroom children are typically divided into groups on a random basis and the performance of each child is evaluated on the basis of how well his group does as a whole. The result is that the best members of each group spend a great deal of time helping the slowest, since by concentrating their efforts where there is the greatest room for improvement they maximize the group's performance and thereby their own grade. Psychologist Urie Bronfenbrenner reported after a recent visit to the Soviet Union that this system appears to generate not only a high degree of motivation on the part of individual students, but generally high morale within groups as well. Specifically, although the slowest members of each group were under pressure to increase their performance, the attitude of the rest of the group was one of enthusiasm and helpfulness rather than criticism (contrary to what one might expect under similar conditions in this country). A critical factor in the successful outcome of this technique would appear to be the strongly held belief that the only reason some members of the group were not doing as well as the others was their lack of equal opportunities as infants and therefore that it was part of the group's obligation to be both supportive and helpful.

While the Russian method meets with considerable success in raising the performance of less able students, thus far it is questionable whether it allows for a concomitant maximization of the abilities of the more gifted children who must spend a significant proportion of their time helping other members of their group. From the standpoint of overall educational output an equalitarian doctrine may be beneficial due to its salutary effect on slower students but less successful in providing opportunities for the highly gifted individual to fully realize his potential. Of course, any such hypothesis is predicated on the assumption that significant differences in capacity do in fact exist between individuals. But regardless of whether we or the Russians are correct about the size of the variance in the distribution of innate abilities in the population and the relative importance of the part played by the learning environment in the development of these abilities, the contrast between Soviet educational techniques and our own points up the potential consequences of taking either extreme position on this issue. To place too great an emphasis on innate capacity is to run the risk of holding expectations that are too low for the bulk of the population and thereby setting limits on output. On the other hand, to neglect the possibility that some individuals are endowed with significantly greater capacities for learning is to jeopardize their opportunities to make the best use of those abilities.

The practical solution to this dilemma would appear to lie somewhere between the two extremes, at least until we have a somewhat more precise notion about the contribution of innate abilities to differences in adult performance. In this country test scores and other measures of intellectual capacity most appropriately should be considered as indicators of the *minimum* level at which the individual is capable of performing, as opposed to the maximum. Such an open-ended approach to intellectual capacity does not preclude the utilization of pedagogical techniques that maximize individual and group motivation, as does the Russian system, and at the same time makes possible the identification of individuals who may require special attention if they are to be stimulated to work up to the limits of their potential.

The mining approach to the development and allocation of manpower has an additional drawback that results primarily from the characteristics of the devices currently used in the discovery of talent. Standardized tests of ability (including those used for the measurement of intelligence, aptitude, and achievement) are useful in predicting academic success, but thus far they have been of more limited value in the prediction of postacademic performance. In addition, correlational data suggest that despite repeated efforts to construct instruments that will facilitate the discovery of qualitatively different kinds of talent, most intellectual ability tests, whether they can be categorized as indicators of intelligence or achievement, measure roughly the same abilities. Thus, the widespread use of such tests in allocating educational and occupational opportunities may have the effect of narrowing the range of available talents and abilities in society's manpower pool. Dael Wolfle, in emphasizing this point, argued that in "the selection and education of persons of ability, it is advantageous for a society to seek the greatest achievable diversity of talent—diversity within an individual, among the members of an occupational group, and among the individuals who constitute a society."[5] To the extent that attempts to predict future performance tend to restrict the range of available talents because of the homogeneity of the instruments used in the predictive process, we must advocate movement away from this position. In a society that is constantly making new demands on its intellectual resources as a result of social and technological change, this point becomes of even greater significance.

In summary, the responsibility of our educational system to maintain a high degree of flexibility in differentiating among students is clear. Not only must schools make a special effort to avoid setting limits on what is expected of individuals, but they have an obligation to provide pupils with a learning environment that will be conducive to the development of the greatest possible variety of skills and abilities. Because of the importance of the part played by the school in influencing an individual's opportunities to develop his abilities and therefore to achieve a higher social status, the pupil is very much at the mercy of the educational system to correctly evaluate his capabilities. From the standpoint of both the society and the individual, it is of critical importance that the school do the best job possible in this regard.

THE MAXIMUM UTILIZATION OF TALENT

A rapidly changing and technologically advanced society creates special problems for those agencies concerned with manpower development and allocation. A complex society demands not only a constant supply of highly-trained manpower but also some means of ensuring that each member of the society ends up in the position for which he or she is best qualified, whether by virtue of innate or acquired abilities. Change has the effect of producing a chronic and almost inevitable state of manpower shortage as job requirements are altered and new positions created. The maximum utilization of available talent is difficult enough at best, but under conditions of rapid social and especially technological change both the training and allocation functions become considerably more complex. These problems raise a number of specific questions for our educational institutions, including (1) what to do about individuals whose skills have become obsolete as a consequence of technological innovations, (2) what to do about individuals whose training has not provided them with any specific skills or professional competence, (3) how to determine what kinds of educational opportunities to offer women in order to increase the contribution of this significant group to the labor force, and finally (4) what to do about those individuals whose innate abilities are not sufficient (for whatever reason one may wish to suggest) to enable them to acquire the complex skills necessary for most of the occupational positions in our society.

THE PROBLEM OF EDUCATIONAL OBSOLESCENCE

The man who finds that his skills are out of date by the time he has finished acquiring them is becoming an increasingly common species as our society becomes technologically more complex and the amount of preparation required for most jobs grows accordingly. An important characteristic of modern occupational life is that the longer a period of training is necessary in order to function effectively in a position, the more vulnerable the individual is to unemployment, or at least to career stagnation, as a result of a change in the nature of the job. The issue here is not only the case where jobs are eliminated through automation but also the case where the job remains but the skills needed to fill it change and the individual discovers that his educational background no longer adequately prepares him to meet the demands of his occupation or profession. The result may not necessarily be a loss of job, but rather a loss of opportunities for advancement or a curtailment of responsibility that represents, in effect, a waste of the individual's training and hard-won skills.

Educational institutions have a responsibility to attempt to mitigate the effects of these changes in the society in at least three different ways. First, educators must pay closer attention to the precise nature of the changes that are taking place and to the effect that they are likely to have on the society's manpower needs. Systematic concern with these questions would make possible more effective counseling throughout the educational system and possibly the introduction of curriculum changes that would anticipate societal demands for new and different kinds of skills. Although it is of course not always possible to predict technological breakthroughs in advance, one can often make fairly accurate guesses by considering which areas are receiving the greatest attention at a given point of time. For example, we may predict the continued growth and applicability of computer technology and a concomitant increase in the already great demand for individuals who are trained in the various skills necessary to this enterprise. It is gratifying to note that in adopting new techniques for teaching mathematics, many school systems have already begun to adapt their curricula to these changes. Up to now, however, educational institutions have been painfully slow for the most part in adapting to the needs of the society. Hopefully, there will come a time when schools, while not losing sight of their responsibilities in the inculcation of basic skills and traditions, will tend to be more sensitive to changes that are likely to have an effect on the appropriateness of the training they are offering or the occupational demands of the society.

Secondly, school systems, as well as the communities they serve, will have to give greater thought to the provision of educational services for the retraining of adults whose skills have become outmoded. Not only must adequate instructional facilities be established, but procedures are necessary for encouraging individuals to take advantage of them. To be successful, adult education, and particularly retraining, requires special techniques on the part of the school. For some groups motivation may be even more of a problem than with teenagers (especially those for whom the loss of jobs has come as a bitter disillusionment), and in all cases critical differences in such variables as the teacher-student relationship make necessary sensitive accommodations to the unique characteristics of the situation. Nevertheless, adult education is a major key to the solution of problems created by a changing society.

Finally, we will have to do a better job of preparing individuals for the eventuality that major retraining or reorientation will be necessary at some point in their adult life. While schools will have to continue to teach pupils specific skills and prepare them for particular occupations, it may be possible to make subsequent readjustments smoother by concentrating on inculcating techniques for learning in addition to specific contents, a point we have considered elsewhere.

THE PROBLEM OF THE GENERALIST VS. THE SPECIALIST

In an age when clerks are being replaced by computers and the liberal-arts-educated junior executive is encountering difficulty in competing with the engineer, the law school graduate, and the specialist in business management, educators as well as students are becoming aware of the problems a specialized society creates for the generalist. In the never ending search for greater efficiency and as a consequence of changes in the nature of the goods and services that are being provided, the trend has been in the general direction of greater organizational size throughout the society. The growing size and complexity of business, industrial, and governmental organizations has resulted in the tendency for most jobs to demand more and more special training on the part of the incumbent. The effect has been to create a situation in which the choice of careers open to the high school student without specialized vocational training or the liberal arts college graduate without professional school credentials or technical experience is increasingly limited. Where positions are open to such individuals the job usually requires that the employee go through a special training program to equip him with the relevant skills.

These changes in the occupational structure of society have had the impact of causing many schools and colleges to institute increasingly specialized curricula and of influencing many students to elect more highly specialized courses of study at the expense of a liberal education in the traditional meaning of the term. College (and even some high school) courses in public relations and advertising, accounting, applied dress designing, life insurance, personnel management, industrial marketing, office procedures, agricultural economics, library science, hotel management, and newspaper typography indicate the extent to which educational institutions have responded to the pressures for a practical and specialized curriculum. Achieving a balance between preparing students adequately for the specialized occupational roles offered by the society and providing them with general intellectual skills that may be of more importance in the long run is not an easy task. The average college student who forsakes a practical curriculum for the liberal arts faces the prospect of having to undertake additional training in order to prepare himself for a desirable career or settling for a position with a relatively uncertain future, for example as a "management trainee" or salesman. For the high school graduate without specialized vocational skills the picture is even darker. The alternatives are an apprenticeship in one of the skilled trades (assuming the individual can gain admittance to the controlling union organization) or a position requiring little or no training other than what can be acquired on job.

As the society becomes more technologically complex we may anticipate that the problem of the generalist vs. the specialist will become more acute. It also seems likely that the society will continue to require individuals who have a broad intellectual background as well as those who have specialized skills. In the manpower market, however, economic factors will continue to play a major role in influencing the kinds of training that will be offered by schools. Two conclusions may be reached regarding the responsibilities of the school and the society in respect to this problem. First, it is of critical importance that the society provide sufficient occupational opportunities for the generalist to encourage some capable young people to pursue a less specialized educational course in its entirety. And second, both schools and college must pay particular attention to providing the specialist with an adequate grounding in the more traditional intellectual skills, including philosophy, writing, mathematics, logic, history, and foreign languages, to enable him to communicate with and appreciate the generalist in taking an effective role in the affairs of his community and the society.

Despite the fact that our society spends almost as much money educating women as it does men, the proportion of women to men in the labor force indicates a return on only a small fraction of this educational investment. Statistically, women do not play a significant part in the industrial, economic, and political life of the society, except as consumers, and they are under-represented in virtually every occupational field (the significant exceptions are, of course, teaching, nursing, and the clerical fields). The talent loss that is represented by the number of well-educated and intelligent women who "retire" from their jobs to devote the remainder of their lives to raising children is very great indeed. The United States Department of Labor reported that in 1962 only 36.9 per cent of all women twenty-five years of age and over were working outside the home, and of those who had completed four or more years of college, nearly half were no longer in the work force. Even in cases where a woman chooses to try to maintain a career, with or without family responsibilities, she must continually deal with the peculiar mixture of resentment and favoritism that results from a general unwillingness to treat a woman like a man, a fear of competition, and our society's firmly held belief that a woman's place is in the home. These factors, combined with the natural impulses of women to bear and raise children, conspire to cause most females in our society to leave the labor force at an early age and not return.

Of course, women do perform a major function in the society (in addition to bearing children) as a consequence of their part in the socialization process. They also frequently fulfill an invaluable supportive function vis-a-vis their husbands. Any major effort to make more efficient use of this pool of talent would necessarily detract from these functions unless some alternative institutional arrangement were to be established. In the Soviet Union women are expected to contribute their skills to the labor force while children, even from a relatively early age, are cared for in communal boarding schools. However, available data on the effects of maternal separation from children indicate rather strongly that although the kind of substitute figure or figures provided in the absence of the mother is of great significance, separation is likely to have deleterious, although usually not irreversible, consequences for the ultimate psychological health of the child.[6] Thus, whether a society can, with an assurance that it will not disrupt the socialization process, encourage the participation of women in the labor force during the childbearing period of their life remains open to question. It will be of particular interest to observe the outcome of Soviet efforts along these lines.

Whether or not any basic change in the institution of the family is contemplated, it does seem likely that somewhat better use could be made of the talents of women in our society. Among the possible ways that this might be accomplished are the following. First, more systematic efforts might be made to encourage women whose children have reached the point where they are less in need of constant maternal support and control to return to work, even though the family might not need the additional income, particularly in positions such as teaching and nursing, where the time and scheduling requirements are somewhat flexible. In the field of education in particular this might be an important source of badly needed teaching personnel, although administrators, school boards, and state certification officers may have to create a special class of positions for such individuals. In addition, since the most likely candidates for such positions will be the college-educated wives of middle- and upper-class business and professional men, it may be necessary for the Federal government to provide income tax exemptions for salaries earned under these conditions in order to make the effort of repreparing oneself for such a position worthwhile. Although women who have been out of touch with the occupational world for several years and who are even farther away from their own educational experiences may not be qualified to take on all of the responsibilities of a full-time career teacher, nurse, or other professional person, special roles might be created to take advantage of whatever capabilities they do possess. Refresher courses and institutes for the updating of previously acquired skills might also be established. As it became more usual for a woman to contemplate moving back into the occupational life of the society as her children attained maturity, this expectation on her part would very likely have the effect of sustaining her interest in her profession and in the maintenance of her skills and talents. Thus not only would the proportion of women participating in the labor force be increased, but the level of competence and vigor of the population as a whole would also be enhanced.

Another way of sustaining interest and making use of the skills of women who are in the process of raising families might be the expansion of a special class of positions designed primarily for the mothers of young children. Specifically, these would be jobs that could be done at home or one or two evenings a week, such as grading papers for full-time teachers, editorial work, and any one of a number of skilled but routine tasks, such as manuscript typing. Some school systems have already instituted programs in which they have elicited the assistance, either on a paid or volunteer basis, of mothers to help overworked teachers with the marking of compositions and other written work. A broad application of these techniques would have the effect of relieving teachers of an enormous amount of routine but time-consuming work and opening up all kinds of possibilities with respect to the kinds of work that might be assigned pupils (for example, more creative writing). It would also dramatically increase the return per unit of teacher time. Utilizing women in this way would also have the benefit of maintaining their interest and competence until such time as they could return to the labor force on a full-time basis.

Finally, more systematic encouragement and guidance might be given to women throughout their educational experience in order to ensure that they acquire the kinds of skills that will be of greatest usefulness to them before, during, and after the period they will be primarily involved in child-rearing. While recognizing that some women prefer to concentrate their efforts on a career in business or a profession instead of raising a family (or even in addition to raising a family in those rare cases of women who can do both), those who are responsible for deciding what kinds of courses shall be offered must face the fact that the majority of the women who graduate from our educational institutions will, at the very least, be dividing their attention between a job and their family. If we are to allow for the importance of the role played by women in the socialization process while at the same time striving to make the best use of the talents of these same women in the labor force, we must make a special effort to provide them initially with the most useful skills, with opportunities to maintain and utilize their abilities while they are raising a family, and, finally, with the motivations that will keep them interested enough in their occupation to return to it when their children have grown up.

THE PROBLEM OF THE INTELLECTUALLY HANDICAPPED

A final educational and social problem that must be solved if we are to achieve the maximum possible utilization of available manpower has been created by the advancing technological sophistication of the society and the consequent increase in the basic intellectual capacities required for the performance of the majority of the roles in the society. Even if innate factors in intellectual capacity are relegated to a minor role in the explanation of individual differences, and most evidence indicates that they have considerably more than a minor influence, one is still faced with the problem of locating jobs for a significant part of the population that does not possess the basic capacity to learn how to manage even a semi-skilled occupational role. Until now there have always been more than enough positions requiring little or no skill and no great capacity for learning to make it possible for most such individuals to earn a reasonable living, given sufficient motivation on their part. But the picture is beginning to change as the number of such individuals increases and the pool of suitable unskilled jobs is simultaneously reduced.

The concern here is not for those individuals who are educationally deprived and who have not had an opportunity to acquire the necessary skills. Upgrading our educational system with particular emphasis on those areas most in need of special facilities and providing means by which capable individuals can get the training they need to qualify for better positions will do much to increase the opportunities of this group. The present focus is on the group of people whose innate intellectual abilities place real limits on their capacity to acquire anything but the simplest skills. As the intellectual requirements for most jobs are raised, the number of individuals whose capacities fall short of the minimum required level can be expected to increase rapidly. Thus far our educational institutions have been relatively ineffectual in helping these individuals to prepare themselves for dealing with our complex society. Except in a few areas where specialists are available in sufficient quantity to provide the kind of individualized attention often needed, schools have tended to try to rid themselves of this problem by sending such children to special institutions. Where this is not possible or, as is usually the case, the degree of retardation is not sufficient to warrant institutionalization, school systems have been concerned only with keeping such children from making a nuisance of themselves and hoping that they will absorb something from their educational confinement. On the one hand, we may be underestimating by a significant margin the capacity of such individuals to acquire basic intellectual skills given the proper educational environment—for example, one that allows for a highly individualized approach to the subject matter. On the other hand, a partial solution to this problem may be achieved by creating a new class of positions in the society for which such individuals would receive specialized training. In any case, up to now most public school systems have not been flexible enough (or had the inclination) to recognize the special educational needs of this group of children and to provide for them in imaginative ways. Steps will have to be taken in this direction, however, if we are to live up to our responsibilities both to the individuals involved and to the broader society.

THE SCHOOL AS A MEANS FOR SOCIAL MOBILITY

The relationship between education and occupational achievement (and consequently social class position) has been demonstrated over and over again in the sociological literature. Despite the fact that some individuals in our society start out with a considerable advantage over others due to differences in family wealth and position, the educational system remains the principal route by which an individual may improve or maintain his social status. A man with little educational background can still rise to a position of power and wealth by dint of hard work, brains, and luck. But the Horatio Algers of the present generation are more likely to have worked their way through four years of college and then graduate or professional school. Not only do most jobs today demand more in the way of specialized training, but the size and bureaucratization of many business and industrial organizations make it much more difficult for the individual who lacks at least the minimum educational qualifications to make his mark on the society.

As we have indicated above, educational institutions influence the level to which an individual may rise in several ways. First and foremost, they provide him with the specific skills that will determine his qualifications for the various careers that the society has to offer. Both the amount of training and the nature of one's educational background are relevant, and as curricula become more specialized at all levels, from the vocational high school to the university, schools can be expected to play an increasingly significant part in determining an individual's career path. The educational setting also provides the first major testing ground for the individual's abilities and energies. One's early academic performance has a lot to do with the opportunities, both educational and occupational, that will be open to him from this point on. The school affords individuals from all racial, ethnic, and class backgrounds an opportunity to show what they can do and thereby earn the chance both to continue their education and eventually to get a job that is commensurate with their abilities and training.

Children learn more than just reading, writing, and arithmetic, or how to operate a drill press in schools. The attitudes they develop toward the society and its institutions (including the school), as well as the social skills they acquire in interacting with their peers, teachers, and other school personnel, are of major importance in determining the kinds of occupational positions to which they will have access. It is for these reasons that civil rights leaders have been so adamant in their denial of the adequacy of attempts to provide compensatory educational facilities for deprived groups as an alternative to systematic or forced integration. Finally, educational institutions contribute some of their own social status to that of their pupils. The graduates of those schools having the best reputations, either academically or socially (or more usually both), seem to have an advantage, however slight, over candidates of equal ability who come from schools having a lower reputation.

We conclude that education is the chief means by which the lower class individual or minority group member may improve his social position. In our achievement-oriented society, although ascribed characteristics of individuals still make a difference in one's chances for success, the school provides an important mechanism that allows high ability and motivation to find its own level in the occupational structure of the society. But the system is not perfect. While statistics show the relationship between education and occupational attainment, they also show clearly the under-representation of the lower socioeconomic groups, children from rural areas, and certain minority groups—principally, Negroes—in colleges and universities. In addition, they indicate the relatively poor performance of members of such groups at lower levels in the educational system. If we assume that real ability is distributed equally among all groups in the society (an assumption which, whether valid or not, is a functional myth for members of the society to hold), then clearly all members of the society do not have equal access to educational facilities limited only by their inherent capacity to benefit from those facilities. Several reasons may be suggested to account for these facts.

(1) The most commonly mentioned reason for the relative lack of educational attainment on the part of members of certain groups in the society is that they are culturally deprived as a result of their social situation and early socialization. It is pointed out, for example, that many such children enter school without having had the advantage of help in learning to read, write, or speak properly from their parents during the preschool years, without the stimulation of constant exposure to books and other cultural objects, and frequently with language problems that make even basic communication with the teacher difficult. Even where the school provides compensatory programs in order to help such children catch up, these efforts tend to be too late and too little to overcome the advantage that children from middle- and upper-class homes already have. Since learning is a cumulative process that depends on a firm grounding in the basic intellectual skills, deprivation in one or more of these fundamental areas has a powerful effect on the individual's rate of progress. On the other hand, the child with fully developed verbal skills is able to proceed at an accelerating pace to take advantage of the advanced training the school has to offer.

There is little doubt that the problem of cultural deprivation is real and that it accounts for a great deal of the relative lack of educational opportunity that members of some groups feel. The solution, however, does not appear to be an easy one. As we have pointed out, compensatory programs, at least of the present type, may not be enough. By the time the child reaches school age, it may be too late to help him catch up to the middle-class child who has had books read to him since he was a year old. We are of course not suggesting that compensatory efforts be abandoned, just that they do not strike at the roots of the problem. The answer seems to lie instead in a major effort to help parents in rural and lower-class urban areas take on some of the responsibility for preparing their children for school. But the difficulties here are very great indeed. For the slum dweller the problems of simply existing from day to day are of considerable proportions and accumulated frustrations and resentment tend to stifle attempts to inculcate anything approaching middle-class values, much less to get mothers to behave in a manner like that of their middle-class counterparts. Some gains might be made by making available to families in rural and slum areas quantities of reading material appropriate for preschool children in the hopes that a sheer increase in exposure to the printed word will have beneficial effects. The mass media, and in particular, television, also provide possible means by which some inroads may be made in cultural deprivation. Finally, an approach which is certain to be tried on a large scale in the not too distant future is the lowering of the age at which children enter school and the establishment of special prekindergarten classes for slum children. It seems likely, however, that unless parental involvement in the educational process can be increased, such programs will have limited effectiveness. In the long run, we may have to wait for the process of generational change to bring about the hoped-for effects.

(2) Closely related to cultural deprivation as a major factor in the differential access of certain groups to educational opportunities is the fact that members of deprived groups often hold attitudes toward educational institutions that are different from those held by the members of the dominant middle- and upper-class groups in the society. The school may be viewed with indifference, suspicion, or even resentment by such groups, and the attitudes of the community are likely to be transmitted and reinforced by a peer culture based on norms diametrically opposed to those of the middle class. The result may be that both educational and occupational aspirations of youth in slum areas or in rural communities will have little relationship to their abilities, or else will be directed toward activities that are in conflict with the goals and norms of the broader society. Sewell finds, for example, that "the educational and occupational plans and aspirations of rural youth—both boys and girls—are quite low in comparison with those of urban youth. This is true not only when we consider the group as a whole, but also when we take into account those in the highly talented third. From all of the evidence, it seems clear that many culturally determined characteristics of the rural youth themselves work against their having high level educational and occupational aspirations."[7] Deutsch finds that in time-samples of classroom activity, from 50 to 80 per cent of all classroom time in elementary schools with predominantly Negro, lower-class children

was "devoted to disciplining and various essentially nonacademic tasks."[8] By comparison, only 30 per cent of classroom time was given over to such activities in elementary schools attended mainly by white children of roughly similar economic status.

Faced with these facts, the peer culture and the influence of home environment on attitudes and aspirations relating to education should be the focus of a major effort on the part of both educators and community workers if we are to make any significant progress in raising the educational level of members of deprived groups in the society.

(3) On the other side of the coin, because most of those who are responsible for the establishment and administration of educational policy are drawn from the middle classes, our educational institutions strongly reflect middle-class norms and values. This tendency is reinforced by the fact that the majority of teachers trace their sociological origins to the dominant groups in the society. Consequently, members of lower-class groups feel (frequently with justification) that they are being unfairly treated by school personnel who do not understand their special problems and who either expect them to conform to middle-class norms (and punish them unsympathetically when they fail) or lower their standards sufficiently so that the more able minority group child is not pushed hard enough. The best teachers also try to avoid assignments to slum schools or transfer to better schools as soon as they have accumulated enough seniority to make a change of position possible. Thus slum schools are typically staffed with less able teachers while the solution of their problems demands the most highly skilled personnel: teachers who are able to adapt to the special needs of the culturally deprived child while at the same time neither lowering their expectations or rejecting the child because of behavior that does not conform to middle-class standards. The problem is summarized as follows by Burton Clark in *Educating the Expert Society:*

> The large and continuing growth of Negro and other dark-skin minority populations in northern cities makes teacher reaction a critical aspect of the education of minorities. The northern urban situation is one in which prejudice alone is not the major factor. It is a matter of the way in which the characteristics (other than skin color and race) of the minority child affect teachers and the operation of the schools. As long as a sizeable share of the children from culturally deprived and lower-class backgrounds are dirty, violent, and unmotivated— *or appear so in the eyes of their teachers*—the teachers are likely to handle them differently, teach them less, and want to escape. The consequence is a lessening of achievement, a low-

ering of opportunity. The problem for the school is to change the "vicious cycle" of interaction between student characteristics and teacher response through such means as increasing the motivation to achieve on the part of the pupils and strengthening the commitment of the best teachers to the worse schools.[9]

An additional means of breaking down the barriers between teachers and students in slum areas is through the increased utilization of teachers who themselves have grown up in such areas and who are familiar with the pressures and counter-pressures, the frustrations and the hostilities of their pupils. A recent study by David Gottlieb[10] indicates that Negro teachers' perceptions of elementary school children in urban slum areas differ markedly from those of white teachers in similar areas. Negro teachers, for example, tended to see the children as "happy," "energetic," and "fun-loving," while the white teachers were likely to see the same children as "talkative," "lazy," and "rebellious." The Negro teachers also expressed greater satisfaction with their current teaching assignment than did white teachers. Several of the large urban school systems, including New York City, are making determined efforts to hire greater numbers of Negro teachers in an effort to increase the communication between the school and the community. But the supply of such teachers can accommodate only a fraction of the need due to the very factors we have been discussing. We can only hope that as advances are made in providing opportunities for members of lower-class, ethnic, and other culturally deprived groups, a large proportion of those who do manage to develop their intellectual skills to the fullest will turn to teaching as the most significant way in which they can contribute to the overall advancement of their group.

(4) Finally, differences in the quality of the educational facilities available to members of various groups in the society contribute materially to varying opportunities for school mobility. The greatest inequalities in educational opportunity occur at the elementary, and to a lesser extent the secondary, level, where the traditional practice of neighborhood schooling coupled with residential segregation, not only along racial lines but with respect to class, religion, and ethnic origin as well, results in wide variation in school quality. Awareness of the importance and extent of the differences between schools in the quality of instruction offered is reflected in the amount of emotion generated on both sides by school integration efforts, in the mass movement of middle- and upper-income families with children of school age to suburban communities in order to ensure that their children will have the best schooling possible, and in the almost frantic demand for private school places by well-to-do parents who

wish to remain in the city or in areas where public schools are not considered to be as good as the private schools.

For the parent who cannot afford (or, because of minority group membership, is unable) either to live in the neighborhood served by the best public schools or to send his children to a private institution, the lack of comparability between schools often means a significant decrement in educational and, consequently, long-range occupational opportunity. That this relative lack of opportunity should be recognized by both children and parents is inevitable; it no doubt contributes to the disillusionment and frustration felt by members of deprived groups. The simple solution to this problem is better schools in slum areas.[11] But the lack of community, student, and teacher morale, shortages of competent teachers, the unwillingness of the best teachers to take positions in schools serving such areas, and the sheer physical and financial problems of providing excellent educational facilities in overcrowded, low-income communities makes the implementation of this solution extraordinarily difficult.

Gains have been made, and it is likely that in the long run many of these problems will be overcome. On the positive side we can point to the increasing reliance on objective tests to uncover hidden talent and to evaluate individual abilities (a form of academic currency that makes it possible for students to overcome the poor reputation of their school), the growing availability of scholarship and loan funds for deserving students, and the appearance of free public education at the college level in the form of junior colleges and state universities. Despite the hopeful signs, however, we are a long way from providing truly equal educational opportunities for all members of the society. Because of the importance of education as a means for social mobility, we must continue to work toward greater availability of educational opportunities, both if we are to live up to the principles on which the society is founded and for the benefit of a society that is increasingly dependent upon a constant supply of highly trained manpower.

•

CHAPTER SEVEN

The School

As a

Formal Organization

•

Several additional variables must be considered if we are to appreciate the many different influences and pressures on the school. These result from its characteristics as a formal organization. In Chapter II we considered some of the social structural aspects of educational institutions: the role relationship between student and teacher, the social system of the classroom and the school, and external influences on each of these social relationships. In the present chapter the discussion will be extended to take into account the effect that *organizational* characteristics of schools and school systems have on the problems created for our educational institutions by a rapidly changing society and their responses to these problems.

As groups become institutionalized (i.e., as they take on functions, specified goals, and a normative structure that give them an existence and continuity independent of the goals and efforts of their members), they acquire a new complex of internal (and external) forces that interact with the groups' goals, its informal social structural characteristics, and the personalities of its members to determine the ultimate nature of the organization. Formal organizational pressures arise at the intersection of function and system, at that point where the instrumental goals of the group (not necessarily of its members) must be translated into action by a particular group of individuals who may or may not already stand in some kind of orderly relationship to one another. As instrumental groups grow in size and complexity, formalized procedures for decision-making, the allocation of responsibility, communication within the group, and the recruitment of personnel become increasingly important if the group is to perform its functions in the most efficient way. Formal organizational characteristics of a group constitute those aspects of its normative structure that are both specified (usually in writing) and which pertain primarily to the way the group is to carry out its functions.

The distinction between social system and organization is by no means a sharp one, since it is obvious that organizational characteristics have a very great influence on the informal social structure of the group and vice versa. System (or social structure) almost never entirely precedes formal organization, although in expressive groups (groups that exist primarily or wholly for the enjoyment of their members and have no goal beyond this) a relatively well-defined set of role relationships (a social system as we have defined it) may exist without any formal organization being introduced. On the other hand, a table of organization and a set of procedures for decision-making, recruitment, communication, and the like may be established for some groups prior to the selection of any personnel. In such a case formal organizational characteristics obviously exist prior to the development of any specific role relationship among the members. The resulting social system to a great extent reflects the formal organization, although informal relationships can be expected to have a modifying impact. In considering the school as a formal organization, we shall want to keep in mind the way the informal social system of the school influences its organizational characteristics and vice versa. Because of its multiple functions and the highly complex network of formal and informal influences from the community, parents, and other groups, this relationship between formal properties and informal relationships turns out to be a major source of problems for the school.

BUREAUCRATIZATION AND THE SCHOOL

Perhaps the most important change that has taken place in American education during the last half century has been the increasing bureaucratization of school systems. We have suggested that the tendency toward organizational formalization along bureaucratic lines has been produced by the increasing size of both individual schools and school systems, along with the greater degree of specialization that is necessary on the part of teachers (and students) as the society becomes more technologically complex. Bidwell points out that "as the school-leaving age has been raised so that most students remain in schools for periods of ten to twelve years, the coordination of educational activities so that they are coherent and sequential moves more and more to the center of school system administration."[1] Since the school is still responsible for the production of a more or less uniform product of a certain minimum quality, the longer the educational process and the more complicated the skills that the school is expected to inculcate become, the more difficult will be the task of making sure the student emerges with the proper qualifications and without undue waste motion. The consequence has been the development of increasingly complex administrative structures within schools and at the system level. This has been necessary to accommodate a growing number of specialists, from the guidance counselor, the school psychologist, and the testing expert to the statistician and the public relations man. As the role of the teacher has become more specialized, recruitment and promotion policies have been formalized, and despite the traditional freedom of the teacher to determine how and what she will teacher her pupils, administrative influence over the activities of teachers has grown significantly, especially in the larger school systems.

Among the responses of school systems to pressures for the provision of more complex educational services and the necessity for the maintenance of greater control over the educational process have been (1) an increasingly fine division of labor, both at the administrative and teaching levels, together with a concern for allocating personnel to those positions for which they are best suited and a formalization of recruitment and promotion policies; (2) the development of an administrative hierarchy incorporating a specified chain of command and designated channels of communications; (3) the gradual accumulation of specific rules of procedure that cover everything from counseling and guidance to school-wide or system-wide testing programs and requirements concerning topics to be covered in many subjects such as history, civics, and social studies; (4) a de-emphasis of personal relationships between students and teachers and between teachers and administrators, and a consequent reorientation towards more formalized and affectively (emotionally) neutral role relationships; and finally (5) an emphasis on the rationality of the total organization and the processes going on within the organization. In general the movement, particularly at the secondary school level, has been in the direction of the rational bureaucratic organization that is typified by most government agencies and many business and industrial firms.

The tendency toward bureaucratization is strongly reinforced by a third layer of influence in the educational hierarchy, that of board members who, in the performance of their fiduciary and managerial roles, exert pressure on administrators to make the best use of limited resources in the same way that corporate directors exercise control over policy. To take an extreme example of the scope of the problems with which school board members and administrators must deal, the annual budget for the New York City School system approaches one *billion* dollars a year, of which upward of $200 million is spent to finance new school construction, over $9 million goes for "executive and business management" and the bill for pupil transportation alone comes to $30 million annually.[2] New York City is a unique case only by virtue of its overwhelming size. Many school districts are currently administering an annual budget comparable to that of a medium-sized corporation. It is only reasonable to expect them to take on many of the characteristics of the latter organizations.

Both administrative and teacher roles have traditionally been defined as professional, and "an important facet of school system organization is the autonomy granted—or perhaps demanded by— the teacher as a professional to make discretionary judgments about procedures to be used during the time a student group is in his charge."[3] Bidwell points out that "both the temporal division of labor and the structural looseness of school systems reinforces the professional basis of school system activities—the discretion of staff members and sub-units to determine what services are to be provided and how this is to be done. But the school system cannot rely entirely on such judgments, since a uniform product must be attained and since the movement of students from grade to grade, and thus from classroom to classroom and school to school within the system must be sequential."[4] As a result of the necessity for an increasing degree of coordination of teaching activities and consequently for increased control over what is to be taught and when, administrative encroachment on the teacher's freedom to exercise his professional prerogatives becomes more frequent. Thus bureaucratization puts additional pressures on the already harassed teacher to make sure that his students meet the standards set for them by the administration. This influence is rationalized as necessary in order to ensure some degree of uniformity in the ultimate product of the educational process and to achieve the greatest amount of coordination and efficiency possible in attaining that objective.

One major way in which control is exercised over the teacher is through the periodic administration of standardized achievement tests that are ostensibly for the purpose of evaluating the progress of individual pupils, but which clearly also serve the function of setting goals for the teacher and providing a standard against which the performance of the class as a whole (and consequently the teacher's effectiveness) may be judged. The effect of this reduction in the autonomy of the teacher role vis-à-vis the administrative staff of the school is to weaken the professional status of the teacher, particularly where teachers are not given a voice in determining what is to go into the curriculum and how it is to be organized.

As school systems grow in size and the skills that must be transmitted become more complex and consequently require a longer period of time to acquire, it may be predicted that administrative attempts to exert control over teachers will be increased and tendencies toward bureaucratization accentuated. Bidwell notes in passing that the effectiveness of administrative controls over teachers is strengthened because the majority (three fourths in 1950) of American teachers are women.[5] He suggests that the actual work involvement of teachers in most schools may be quite low, since women are likely to be more concerned with extraorganizational roles than with their position as teacher and male teachers more oriented to promotion into the administrative echelons than to competing with their female colleagues. If so, Bidwell points out that "colleague relations and norms typically may be weak among teaching staffs, tipping the balance of power in school systems to the administrators and school boards."[6]

One reaction on the part of teachers to bureaucratization of the school system has been the sporadic growth of teachers' unions. Up to now the two major organizations representing teachers, the National Education Association and the American Federation of Teachers (a CIO-affiliated union organization), have had only a superficial impact on educational policies and practices relating to teachers, according to a report prepared for the National Society for the Study of Education by Myron Lieberman.[7] But it is of considerable interest that the New York City school system, the largest and probably the most bureaucratized system in the country, alone has had to contend with a strong union organization, one that has been willing to act like a union even to the extent of striking to get higher salaries. One third of the membership of the American Federation of Teachers is in six big cities where school systems are most likely to be bureaucratic in form and operation. From the fragmentary evidence available thus far it would appear that the growth and development of teachers' unions as truly influential bargaining agents in American education will coincide with a lessening of teacher autonomy and an increase in the degree of control exerted by administrators over the teacher role (and possibly vice versa). It remains to be seen what effect unionization will have on the professionalization of the teacher role, although to the degree that professionalization requires freedom from direct administrative control (even though the boundaries of this control have been bargained for) it would seem to be reasonable to argue that unionization would have the effect of weakening the professional status of teachers.

BUREAUCRATIZATION AND THE TEACHER-STUDENT RELATIONSHIP

A decrease in the degree of autonomy granted teachers creates some special problems for school systems due to the characteristics of the client group served by the school—its students—and the necessary adaptations that teachers must make to this group in order to fulfill their role obligations. The student group is unique in that below the university level it is recruited involuntarily and without reference to achievement (except in the case of some private schools and a few specialized public secondary schools). In addition, as Bidwell points out, the central activities of the student role are not directly relevant to the immediate interests or lives of its incumbents. For the most part students have little choice about whether they will attend school or where, and the school has little option in deciding who it will admit. As a result, "the school bureaucracy and its staff confront a client society characterized by values and patterns of activity at best irrelevant to the service goals of the school, more likely opposed."[8] Some of the characteristics of the peer culture have been examined above, and its influence on student attitudes concerning academic achievement has been clearly documented in studies such as Coleman's, which was discussed above. Because the behaviors demanded of students by the school have little immediate relevance to the central problems of adolescents in our society—for example, learning how to deal with members of the opposite sex and achieving independence from adult authority while at the same time beginning to acknowledge the responsibilities that go with independence—, the activities and abilities that are highly valued in adolescent subculture seldom correspond to those that are valued by the school. It may be that the anxiety of parents, teachers, and guidance counselors over the increased competition to get into college (especially a prestige school) will be reflected in a change in the saliency of academic achievement in the peer culture. Even if this were to take place, however, it would affect only that relatively small number of highly able students for whom academic achievement is already a significant value.

Bidwell notes that in the face of a student society in which the major incentives of peer esteem and acceptance are manifested in allegiance to student leadership and a well-defined and firmly held system of norms, teachers tend to respond less to ability variation among their students than to variations in students' social power or personalities in an effort to channel the more salient social motivations of students into academic pursuits. The teacher is therefore unable to maintain bureaucratically defined impersonal role relationships with students (whether or not the teacher desires this type of relationship) because maintenance of control over the student sub-

culture requires a particularistic adaptation toward individual students. The resolution of this conflict in the teacher role is more of a
problem at the secondary level since, according to Parsons,[9] the
teacher-student relationship in high school is supposed to be more
impersonal and bureaucratic than in elementary school (more teaching of moral values and the like goes on at the elementary level)
and since student society tends to be more closely knit at the secondary level.

There would appear to be no simple way out for the teacher
who is caught between bureaucratic administrative demands and the
problem of dealing with a student society, the members of which
perceive their relationship to the school in a quite different way.
The traditional accommodations of the school to student society have
been the use of extracurricular activities to contain the social life of
students and to co-opt student social structure (for example, by coerc-
ing popularly chosen student leaders to assist in motivating their
peers to participate in academic activities) and short-run attempts by
teachers to disrupt the student social system with such official sanctions as grades and detentions or, as we have indicated, through the
use of affective interaction with students. The first of these techniques often produces dysfunctional consequences for the school and
reinforces the solidity of the student society. It also tends to focus
the interest of parents and other adults in the community on nonacademic accomplishments of students, thus weakening their commitment to educational pursuits. The use of official sanctions to enforce
adherence to school norms and motivate students to participate in the
main activities of the school can only be really effective where the
rewards and penalties used are perceived as important by students.
If getting high grades adds nothing to an individual's status (or even
reduces it) in the student society, there is little reason for him to
study any harder than is necessary to stay in school or perhaps if
he has college aspirations, meet the minimum standards for a nearby
state college. With the development of junior college systems that are
open to all high school graduates, as in California, he need not even
jeopardize his long-range chances for high level graduate or professional training, since a good record during the first two years at a
junior college will qualify him to transfer into a four-year college of
solid academic standing. As long as status in a peer society that
values social skills, appearance, wealth, or athletic ability more than
school grades remains the most important thing in the life of the
secondary school student, it is highly unrealistic to expect a bureaucratic reward system to have a significant impact on his motivational
pattern.

Many teachers resort to attempts, whether directly or indirectly,
to establish an affective relationship with students in order to pro-

vide a basis for personal appeals for them to increase their motivation to study or behave themselves. In so doing, the teacher often finds it necessary to direct his attention toward those students possessing the greatest social power, since it is this commodity that counts most in the student society's marketplace. Sooner or later under these conditions circumstances are likely to arise in which the teacher is forced to compromise educational goals in order to maintain particularistic relationships with individual students or to avoid incurring the hostility of those members of the student society holding the greatest influence over their peers. This situation becomes more serious as the conflict between student norms and institutional norms increases, thus lessening the effectiveness of organizational sanctions such as grades. A good example of the latter process may be seen in the means that are frequently used by substitute teachers in attempting to maintain control over an unruly classroom. Under these conditions even minimum bureaucratic sanctions such as fear of punishment for misconduct are lessened due to the fact that the substitute teacher may not know students' names and, more important, may be reluctant to call on the administration for help since this would reflect on the substitute's professional abilities. The result is frequently overt favoritism and a willingness on the part of the teacher to bargain away special privileges in return for the cooperation and assistance of the leaders of the student group in maintaining some degree of control over the situation.

Comparable compromises of educational goals are often encountered in slum schools where teachers may find that institutional rewards and punishments have little or no meaning at all for pupils. The situation tends to be complicated further in large cities by the fact that school systems in these places have been most subject to bureaucratization, and therefore as organizations are likely to be least flexible in adapting to the special motivational problems presented by a client group that shares none of the institution's values or goals. The effect of this conflict between organizational characteristics and student norms may be the virtual collapse of the educational system in such areas unless some way can be found to integrate the conflicting value systems without sacrificing the integrity of institutional goals, an extraordinarily difficult problem under conditions of high bureaucratization.

Two alternative adaptations to the lack of congruence between school and student goals may be proposed. First, it may be possible to modify the curriculum in such a way as to make classroom activities correspond more closely to immediate interests and values of students, while at the same time maintaining a focus on institutional goals. To take a frequently used example, more meaningful and relevant concrete examples of the operation of scientific principles such as internal combustion in an automobile engine or the growth and development of the human organism might be used. At a subtler level, a more persistent and conscientious effort might be made to relate concepts and ideas derived from literature, social studies, history, economics, and civics to the problems being faced by students in the management of their own lives. Although there is no doubt that good teachers everywhere already make use of this technique in arousing the interest of their students, considerably more systematic attention needs to be devoted to developing new ways of dramatizing the fact that intellectual activity does not have to be divorced from the problems of the real world.

Suppose, for example, that in addition to the traditional examples of the usefulness of the scientific method (Louis Pasteur, the discovery of the cause of yellow fever, and the like), students were encouraged to take a systematic look at some aspect of their own behavior or the activities of their peer group under more or less controlled conditions and with a hypothesis or two about the outcome (perhaps derived from something studied in English literature). Although considerably more difficult to handle, this technique would have the distinct advantage of demonstrating the usefulness of an intellectual tool for helping us understand our own behavior and the behavior of others. If it is assumed that a major concern of the student society is with interpersonal relations, including such things as the acquisition of status and prestige and the resolution of conflict within groups, then a scientific analysis of these processes would have great salience for students. We would also predict that the halo from their increased interest in the above-mentioned project might result in a closer attention to more traditional approaches to the subject.

Two factors are of course involved in making one's subject matter "come alive" to students: an intimate knowledge of the topic in both abstract and real terms and, even more important, a more than skin-deep sensitivity to the characteristics and needs of one's students that makes possible an awareness of the points of contact between the subject and the experience of the pupil. It is the latter requirement that causes so many classes to flounder on the shoals of lack of communication between teacher and student, especially where the background of the teacher is very different from that of his students. Greater numbers of teachers are needed who themselves have grown up in slum areas and who are better able to understand some of the conditions and often conflicting pressures under which their students must exist. But this does not appear to be the whole answer to the problem, since the need for competent teachers in low income and rural places far exceeds the current capacity of these same areas to produce teaching personnel. Until such time as the vicious cycle between poverty and low educational attainment can be broken, we will have to concentrate on helping new teachers, whatever their background, to better understand the particular problems their students must face daily.

A second potential educational response to an indifferent adolescent subculture is the development and utilization of teaching methods designed especially to capitalize on the existence of a student society. Without compromising educational goals it may be possible to discover ways of manipulating the social structure of the student group —for example, through such simple techniques as altering a classroom seating arrangement, by changing existing communication patterns so as to undermine the effectiveness of a hostile student leader, or by appointing the leader to a position of responsibility in regard to the primary activities of the school. The aim would be at least to reduce the negative impact of the student society on the school and at best to use its influence to channel students' interests in useful directions. In this respect the Russian technique of emphasizing competition between groups of students in the classroom is instructive.

The difficulty, of course, is making sure that the student society serves the interest of the school and not vice versa. This requires both sophistication and firmness on the part of school personnel, since it may be anticipated that students will strongly resist any attempts by the school to interfere with their groups. Abortive attempts at such manipulation are likely only to increase the cohesiveness as well as the hostility of student society. On theoretical grounds it may be suggested that teachers or administrators should avoid any actions that may be perceived as threatening by the adolescent society, and particularly its leaders, *unless* the school personnel involved possess sufficient administrative weapons and are prepared to destroy the existing society entirely.

One of the things that is indicated by the foregoing discussion is the need for a greater emphasis in teacher training institutions on the subculture of the adolescent society and, in particular, on the ways in which the teacher might be able to capitalize on the interests of that society's members in presenting his subject matter. Unfortunately, social scientists still don't know as much about adolescents and their social groups (especially when social-economic status and ethnic background vary) as we will need to know in order to maximize the salience of the educational experience. But we have more information than we are currently using. Intensive collaboration between social scientists and educators in the matter of curriculum adaptations to a hostile or indifferent student society would very likely produce some significant strides forward, both with regard to method and to content. Teachers also must be given more systematic help in empathizing with their students, particularly in those critical areas where the normative prescriptions and proscriptions of the community, as well as of the student group itself, are likely to diverge significantly from those with which the teacher is familiar.

In all of these endeavors we are going to have to be considerably more creative than we have been in the past. Up to now educators have been reluctant to face up to the embarassing facts of student indifference, lack of motivation, and often outright hostility. The attitude of teachers and administrators alike has been that it is up to the students to alter their feelings about the school rather than for the school to take the initiative in attempting to change the student; that it is improper for the school to "water down" its curriculum or try to "sugar-coat" the subject matter in order to get pupils to pay attention. To the extent, however, that institutional sanctions are ineffective in altering the motivational pattern of students who are primarily oriented toward the reward system of their own society, the "get tough" solution of educational conservatives may not provide enough of an answer to the problem. It seems fairly clear that the existing reward and punishment system of the school will work to the extent of ensuring the minimum performance necessary to stay in school, especially for children from the middle and upper classes, for whom staying in school is a significant value that is reinforced by both family and the community culture. But except for a relatively small group of prestige college oriented children, the evidence is that it will not provide much of an increment to motivation over this minimum level. This is especially true for those children who are imbedded in a student (and community) subculture that is indifferent to the school and its goals.

The conclusion is inescapable that the school must assume some part of the responsibility for raising the motivational level of the majority of students unless we are willing to continue to let the educational level of the society as a whole be determined by the values and interests of an adolescent subculture that, by virtue of its dependent yet independent and functionally irrelevant status, is structurally isolated from the mainstream of the society and consequently from the dominant cultural values. Likewise, our teacher-training institutions and the academic community in general will have to acknowledge their part in solving these problems if we are to move forward significantly in the area of student motivation. Social scientists will have to give more attention to such questions as the origin and dynamic properties of children's peer groups, educators will have to learn how to translate what we know about such groups into educational practice, and teachers will have to learn to recognize when new approaches are necessary.

The necessity for accomplishing all of this within an increasingly bureaucratic context adds to the apparent difficulties. The foregoing suggestions require the capacity for a degree of flexibility that already may be beyond the reach of many school systems, particularly those in large urban areas. A major task facing most school systems would appear to be full-scale reassessment of administrative policies in order to make sure that they have provided for the maximum degree of flexibility and innovation, along with a degree of professionalization of the teacher role that is consistent with external demands for uniform standards against which pupil progress and attainments may be measured.

Although bureaucratization may tend to inhibit innovation at the lower levels, it should be noted that in some situations a bureaucratic form of organization may enhance the capacity of a school to deal effectively with its problems. An efficient formal administrative structure makes possible rapid dissemination of a new procedure or curriculum change throughout the system, thereby giving the system as a whole a striking power not shared by more decentralized organizations. Thus, if effective techniques can be found for dealing with student groups, a bureaucratically organized system offers unique advantages in getting them into practice quickly. But bureaucratic communication systems are best suited for disseminating simple regulations and procedures, not relatively complicated and sophisticated techniques requiring judgment and initiative on the part of the individual (in this case the teacher) who is to put them into effect. Most ways of dealing with student groups are of the latter type. The result is that we are again confronted with a basic conflict between the rigidity that is a part of bureaucratic communication and the demands of the teacher-student relationship for a context that permits a high degree of flexibility. In the long run the solution would seem to lie in a compromise that permits both some degree of administrative control over the teacher, perhaps based primarily on the use of standardized tests, and yet allows for the increased professionalization of the teacher role, including the freedom to adapt teaching methods to fit the demands of the situation. It is clear that a major factor in the creation of such an administrative-teacher balance of power will be the extent to which training of teachers is upgraded, thus providing a sufficient number of professionally oriented and competent teachers to make it possible for administrators to rely on the teacher's ability to adapt to the demands of the situation without losing control or compromising the school's goals.

PERSONNEL—THE PROBLEM OF PROFESSIONALIZATION

Perhaps the single most critical organizational problem facing most schools today is a shortage of well-trained teachers. The teaching function is the foundation of the educational process and the effectiveness of our schools depends primarily on the training, experience, and devotion of the classroom teachers who must take responsibility for actually dealing with students. The current lack of competent teachers is felt by virtually all schools, even those in the wealthy and prestigious communities where teaching is highly rewarded. But the shortage attains massive proportions in those areas most in need of the best teaching personnel—low-income urban and rural areas. At the source of this problem are a number of factors: the rapid population growth that has filled classrooms faster than they can be built (59,800 classrooms were scheduled for completion in 1963-1964)[10]; low salaries that make it difficult to attract men into the field; competing interests of women that result in a high rate of job turnover and a relatively low proportion of experienced personnel anywhere; poor working conditions, especially in low-income and slum areas; heavy teaching loads and rebellious pupils who take the fun and satisfaction out of the job; and, finally, the fact that the most successful teachers, in particular the males, find themselves drawn into administrative positions in the bureaucracy in deference to the differential prestige of administrative as opposed to teaching positions. As in so many similar situations, the various factors tend to reinforce one another, thus making significant gains extremely difficult to achieve, especially in the most critical areas. Many aspects of educational personnel problems have already been considered at length; however, one or two additional comments on the question of professionalization of the teacher role may be in order in the light of the foregoing discussion of current changes in the organizational characteristics of school systems.

Any major strengthening of the teaching profession will depend in large part on the degree to which the overall career commitment of teachers can be increased in order to make possible an upgrading of teacher training (along the lines suggested in the previous section as well as in subject matter competence), to attract more and better candidates (and especially men) into the field and to cut down somewhat on the extremely high rate of turnover currently characteristic of the profession. In a recent questionnaire study of a national sample of beginning teachers,[11] it was found that relatively few new teachers intended to stay in teaching until retirement and 51 per cent did not expect to be teaching five years later. A large proportion of the women expected to leave teaching at least temporarily for homemaking responsibilities, indicating that for them their sex role was dominant over their occupational role, as one might expect. On the other hand, many men hoped to move from classroom teaching into administrative and supervisory positions, also indicating a lack of commitment to the teaching profession as well as an awareness of differences in prestige (at least for men) between teaching and administration.

Major differences in degree of commitment to the teaching profession as well as perceived status and satisfaction with one's position have also been noted between elementary, junior high, and high school teachers. One study conducted by the State Department of Education in New York noted that the work of many junior high school teachers appeared to be essentially a transient occupation. Of all the teachers covered by the study, "only a third set out specifically to teach at this level, almost half expressed doubt that they would choose it if given another chance, and fewer than half planned to stay in junior high teaching until retirement."[12] Furthermore, junior high teachers tended to perceive their own job less favorably than they viewed senior high school teaching, and they commonly felt that they had less opportunity (compared with the high school teacher) to teach what they knew, with less assurance of the academic importance of their work (although they typically had a high estimate of its social significance in the sense that it involves greater responsibility for and involvement in the overall development of pupils).

Similarly, there would appear to be significant differences in the degree of professional commitment of elementary school teachers as compared with either junior high or senior high school teachers, a tendency that is reinforced by the fact that in most states higher educational standards are maintained for certification at the secondary level than at the elementary level. These factors, along with some previously mentioned characteristics of the teacher role in American society, including the tendency for parents to place the teacher (and the school, for that matter) in a service relationship to the family and the growing degree of administrative control over teaching, weaken the professional status of teachers as a group.

As long as a large proportion of those who are involved in teaching perceive their occupation as merely temporary and a stepping stone to a more desirable goal—in the case of women, marriage and a family; in the case of men, an administrative position in the educational hierarchy—any significant progress in upgrading the quality of teaching generally, and in particular in those areas most in need of improvement, will be extremely difficult to make. Lack of professional commitment means that many potential teachers are less likely to be willing to undertake particularly rigorous and extensive training or to take the trouble to make more than a perfunctory effort to upgrade their skills while on the job. It also means that the most capable and ambitious individuals—both men and women—will be drawn into more highly professionalized positions such as counseling and guidance instead of teaching.

There are, of course, many professionally committed and extremely capable teachers who would at least think twice before leaving their teaching post to take an administrative position. But such individuals are in the minority. With the exception of the legendary dedicated teacher of the poor, they tend to be found in the smaller, less bureaucratized school systems serving middle- to high-income communities that can afford to pay well for good teaching both in monetary and prestige terms. One of the barriers to professionalization of the teacher role is that there are relatively few financial and status rewards for the outstanding and experienced teacher as compared to the ill-prepared novice. Although school systems have been slowly recognizing the necessity to extend the upper end of their pay scale to reward advanced training, experience, and even merit, thus far typical increments in salary even in the best schools do not begin to do justice to the contribution made by the exceptional teacher. The inadequacy of opportunities for professional advancement as long as one remains a teacher is probably a major factor in the inclination of men who must support families to gravitate toward administrative positions or, more likely, to avoid education as a career altogether.

Raising the quality of teaching and consequently the professional commitment of teachers under conditions of inadequate rewards, increasing bureaucratization, and difficult working conditions looks like an almost impossible task, at least without some major re-evaluation on the part of society to commit a larger share of its resources to education. Federal aid to education may be one solution to the problem. Or communities and state agencies may be persuaded to spend significantly greater sums on their schools. In one sense it is encouraging to note that with respect to the balance of power between the school's administrative bureaucracy and its teaching staff the situation may be self-correcting. With increased competence, adequate rewards, and thereby status on the part of teachers there is almost certain to be a tendency towards greater teacher autonomy and consequently a more professional orientation to the task at hand. Until these steps are taken, however, we cannot expect much relief for the personnel problems of our schools.

COMMUNICATION

As the size of school systems and individual schools increases, communication within the organization becomes more of a problem. Bureaucratization implies, in addition to a greater specialization of roles, a hierarchical ordering of positions and a formalization of channels of communication between positions in the system. In city school systems the superintendent of schools may be separated from principals by one or more layers of administrative authority. Teachers are less likely to have easy access to administrative personnel other than their immediate supervisor (who may be a department

chairman or at best an assistant principal) or specialized staff personnel with whom they share responsibility for a particular group of
students. Under these conditions communications at all levels
becomes routinized, frequently taking the form of mimeographed
memoranda or formal administrative directives circulated to all personnel at a given level in the hierarchy. Not only is the degree of
flexibility in the organization's response to problems decreased by this
formalization of communication, but teacher morale and identification with the aims of the system as a whole may be adversely
affected.

Much depends, of course, on the extent to which local units in
the system are autonomous from the overall administrative super-
structure of the district and consequently on how much freedom
individual principals have to make adaptations, set school policy and
change administrative procedures in order to maximize teacher
morale and motivation in their own particular situation. Where sufficient local autonomy is lacking, the rigidity of formalized transmission of policy and procedures from the system level to the school
is likely to result in a decrease in teacher initiative and innovation
with respect to teaching methods and a consequent lack of creative
enthusiasm on the part of teachers and other local personnel. Obviously, complete freedom to set policy, change methods, and the like
cannot be permitted local personnel if the superintendent of schools
is expected to assume responsibility to the board of education for
educational policy. The problem is to arrive at a point of balance
between complete dependence on the formal specification of policy
over increasingly complex communication channels and the abdication of responsibility for policy on the part of system personnel. The
necessity for an efficient feedback mechanism to permit principals and
teachers to effectively question system-wide policy as applied to their
situation is clearly indicated. Given the vast diversity of student problems and the even greater range of teacher-pupil relationships, it is
also of critical importance that some slippage be encouraged despite
the fact that a lack of rigid administrative regulation will occasionally
result in embarrassment (or parental harassment) for system officials.

A major theme of this book has been that a rapidly changing
society requires of its educational system a high degree of sophistication in the adaptation of teachers to the changing needs of pupils
and to a subject matter that literally may be altered overnight as a
result of a new discovery or technological breakthrough. The transmission (much less the development) of specific policies and procedures of sufficient sophistication and subtlety to provide for all of
the conceivable contingencies that are likely to be faced by teachers
and local administrators is difficult enough under conditions of face
to face interaction over a period of time. It is a virtual impossibility

given only formal channels of communication and the necessity for uniform policy throughout the system. A good example is the very great difficulty in communicating necessary information about standardized tests to teachers who must administer them and make intelligent use of scores in a system-wide testing program. If our large school systems are to live up to their responsibilities to the society, administrators at all levels must do some hard thinking about providing ways to circumvent formal channels and to facilitate intimate and immediate communication throughout the system when it is needed; or else significantly increase the autonomy of local units.

ALLOCATION OF RESOURCES

Every group or organization must provide for the allocation of its available resources in order to accomplish its aims. Except in imaginary utopias these resources, both material and human, are nearly always scarce relative to the needs of the organization. The process of allocation therefore involves the establishment of some form of priority as to which of the competing demands should be filled first and, if an unequal division is to be made, which deserves the greater share. For school systems that are typically confronted with an even greater scarcity of resources relative to their needs than many other organizations in the society, these decisions present a major administrative problem. To consider in any detail the process by which resource allocation is accomplished in various types of school systems and the problems that result from the different means is not possible here. However, one major dimension of the overall problem is worth our consideration.

In broadest terms educational resources (primarily tax revenues) are allocated either to pay the salaries of personnel or to provide the physical facilities necessary for the operation of the school system, including buildings, desks, textbooks, language laboratories, paper clips, and chalk. Personnel expenditures may be broken down further into those funds allocated for support personnel (guidance counselors, principals, testing specialists, secretaries, janitors, superintendents, and the like) and those spent for teachers' salaries. Similarly, although perhaps less clearly, the funds provided for physical facilities may be divided into those spent on things that are absolutely necessary for the functioning of the school in its most essential form— for example, classrooms, fuel to heat the classrooms in winter (but not air conditioning for summer), and textbooks—and, on the other hand, those that are expended for facilities that may enhance the basic educational experience but are not absolutely necessary for it— for example, cafeterias, gymnasiums, auditoriums, swimming pools, published standardized tests, language laboratories, closed circuit

television, and band uniforms. The absolute fundamentals are represented by the one-room schoolhouse staffed by a single teacher (no
physical "frills," no support personnel), whereas the opposite extreme
is the modern general high school, staffed with guidance counselors
and nurses, and complete with air conditioning and whirlpool baths
for the football team.

Funds that are expended for nonessential physical facilities or
administrative personnel are, of course, not available for teachers
or textbooks. Deciding where to draw the line between the essential
and the nonessential, the necessary parts of the educational process
and the "frills" that make the task easier or more pleasant for
teachers and students alike, has become a major part of the job
of school superintendent and the local board of education. Often
the distinction between what is "necessary" and what is "desirable
but unnecessary" becomes less than clear in this process. In analyzing the factors that typically go into the solution of this problem,
along with broad trends in the allocation of educational resources
in this country, two things become clear. First, no one really knows
where the line ought to be drawn. The advantages of musical instruments, gymnasiums and cafeterias are obvious, but at what point
should funds be diverted from teacher salaries or the provision of
classrooms to these purposes. Second, whatever the optimum balance
from the educational standpoint might be, the trend has been strongly
in the direction of *relatively* more funds being allocated to "soft" or
secondary functions as compared with sixty years ago. In addition
to such statistics as the number of school counselors per secondary
school, whatever doubts the reader might have about this would be
immediately dispelled were he to venture into the main exhibit
hall at the Annual Meeting of the American Association of School
Administrators, where manufacturers of everything from bleacher
seats to automated record-keeping systems vie for the attention of
school purchasing agents. One reason for this has been the sheer
growth in the size of school systems as administrative units. It is a
fact of organizational life that large organizations must allocate a
relatively greater proportion of their personnel resources to non-
productive support functions (administrative, clerical, service, et
cetera) than smaller organizations. Another reason is that physical
facilities such as the school plant are highly visible and tend to be
used as measures of the quality of the system, although the correlation here is highly unreliable. School board members and tax payers
are more likely to be persuaded to spend their money on things
they can see.

The best answer is to make sufficient funds available to our
school systems to enable them to do both—to pay high enough
salaries to attract (and hold) capable teachers as well as to provide

all of the peripheral services and facilities that have come to be expected of our schools. The wealthiest school systems come fairly close to this ideal, though perhaps few superintendents of schools (and even fewer teachers) would be willing to admit it. Even the best-heeled systems still pay salaries that are only high enough to draw the better teachers away from other areas but not enough to increase substantially the likelihood of encouraging more able individuals to enter teaching as a career. In the majority of cases we are far from achieving such a goal. As school systems become more bureaucratized and until adequate resources become available for all purposes, administrators and parents alike are going to have to live with the distinctions made above and their implications for educational budgets. Perhaps we are spending too much money on secondary activities and facilities and not enough on the main enterprise.

This issue strikes at the very roots of most current controversy over education, since its analysis requires a specification of educational goals as well as a ranking of these goals according to their value in hard dollars, both to the community and the society. It is not surprising that educators and politicians alike have been glad to steer clear of it thus far. How long the problem can be ignored remains to be seen, but growing pressure from minority groups for increased educational services with emphasis on more and better teachers and more classrooms is certain to focus new attention on the issues just raised. We can only hope that those who are responsible for decisions on these issues will have the courage and intelligence to phrase the debate in the foregoing terms instead of succumbing to the ever present pressures from commercial and other nonprofessionally interested parties. As long as the resources available for educational purposes are scarce, the vitality of our schools depends to a large extent on their wise and considered disposition.

•

CHAPTER EIGHT

The Role of the School

in an

Emerging World Community

•

Ours is not the only society in the world today that is changing. Many nations are undergoing far more rapid technological, political, and social change than the United States; these societies face many of the same kinds of difficulties in adapting to change that we do, except often in even greater profusion and with a greater sense of urgency. In addition to the internal problems it produces for any society, change has become the common denominator in any equation that forms the basis for the emergence of a world community composed of all manner of political units, cultures, and peoples. Worldwide communication facilities, new means of transportation, international commerce, and the increasingly rapid spread of knowledge (as well as beliefs and ideologies) have created an unprecedented and almost instantaneous interdependence and unity among nations. We are on the threshold of a new age in the history of the world: an era in which, for many intents and purposes, all of the peoples of the world will have to be viewed as members of a single society. It will no longer be possible for a single nation, no matter how powerful or how insignificant, to ignore completely any of the other members of the world community, or for her citizens, either individually or collectively, to act without regard for the impact of their actions on the citizens of other nations. Almost overnight the nature of the world has changed dramatically, from a collection of relatively independent and semi-autonomous societies to a group of peoples who, though still separate politically, are inextricably bound together culturally and socially through the mechanisms of mass communication, trade, and technological development.

From an educational standpoint these developments are of critical importance. No longer is the primary function of our schools merely the socialization of members of American society, but the socialization of potential members of a world society as well. Increasingly, Americans will have to be able to communicate with citizens of other nations on an individual basis and collectively through our national foreign policies. As individuals we must have a sufficient grasp of the history, customs, and language characteristics of the societies with which we must deal to behave sympathetically, intelligently, and consistently. As a nation we are beginning to accept the impracticality of isolationism in an age of world trade and ideological colonialism. Similarly, the dangers of ethnocentrism, the belief that one's own way of doing things is always best, are becoming apparent as more Americans travel abroad and we are forced to acknowledge the accomplishments of nations with which we differ politically and culturally.

In a totalitarian nation where only members of the ruling elite and other special groups are permitted to travel outside the boundaries of the society, an educated and cosmopolitan citizenry is more of a handicap than an advantage. Only those who are in positions of responsibility for the development and execution of foreign policy need have a sophisticated grasp of the intricacies of world affairs. In a democratic society such as our own, however, the common man frequently plays an important role in determining the ultimate course of national policy. Not only are those who are charged with the conduct of our foreign affairs chosen by the total society, but their responsibility to the people does not end with the counting of the votes. Instead, it continues on a day-to-day basis until the next election, when our leaders are very much subject to recall if their actions are not to the liking of the members of the society. Thus, although national foreign policy may be generated and implemented by specialists, its substance and consequences are subject to approval by the common man. And those who create it are aware of this fact.

The failure of the United States Congress to agree on support for the League of Nations in 1919 reflected at least in part the effective lack of concern of members of the society with international affairs and the widespread fear of involvement in entangling alliances. The shift that has taken place in this point of view is clear in the current willingness of Congress to continue to provide a disproportionate share of the financial support of the United Nations. But undercurrents of disagreement can be discerned in many quarters. The instability of the present situation may be seen in the vitality of conservative political movements that advocate at least a much harder line in our foreign policy and at most a return to virtual isolationism, this time based on massive nuclear defense capabilities. The outcome of the current debate over foreign policy is likely to depend on a number of factors, not least of which will be the actions of Communist bloc nations and allies such as Britain and France. But in any case the attitudes of the American people, as reflected in the choices of elected officials, can be expected to have a significant effect on our formal policies vis-à-vis other nations as well as our more informal attitude toward the rest of the world, friends and foes alike.

Without becoming involved in a discussion of the relative merits of various points of view concerning American foreign policy, it seems highly unlikely that we shall ever again be able to entirely avoid active participation in the world community of nations. For one thing we can no longer be indifferent to conflicts anywhere in the world, since with the spread of nuclear arms the smallest disturbance can escalate into a war of total destruction. This will become increasingly possible as more nations join the "nuclear family." Even if it were desired, we could not avoid continued involvement in the emerging communication network (to which we have thus far been the major contributor) that will soon make possible an infinitely greater degree of culture contact through the mass media and consequently a kind of worldwide acculturation.

The struggle for power among nations goes on unabated, but it has been transferred to a new arena—the battleground of persuasion and public opinion, where the weapons are ideas rather than guns, although their effect may be no less deadly. The more unthinkable armed conflict becomes (as a consequence of the development of increasingly devastating weapons), the more important will become the ideological warfare which has replaced it. Given the continued avoidance of a nuclear holocaust and assuming that no immediate way will be found to resolve our ideological differences with other nations, the continuance with increased intensity of the battle for men's minds would appear to be inevitable. More than in any struggle in history, the key to winning this battle would appear to be knowledge on the part of the members of the society.

In this conflict the responsibility of our public educational system is clear. More than ever before the school must recognize its broader role in regard to the world outside our national boundaries. The teaching of American or even European history, for example, is no longer enough if our citizens are to begin to have an understanding of the forces and occurrences that have created our competition for world leadership. The emergence of Africa as a collection of independent and potentially powerful nations and the increasingly important role in world affairs being played by Communist China are only two examples of the many changes that have added critical new dimensions to the complex blend of power and influence that determines the course of international politics. If we are to create a truly educated citizenry, one that is capable of guiding its elected officials toward a responsible foreign policy in this changing world, more emphasis will have to be given to the history and culture of these new nations in our school curricula.

Although there is some evidence that English is coming into use as an international language, at least in some parts of the world, it will be a long time before this will be a means by which Americans will be able to communicate readily with the peoples of most nations. As new countries join the world community as active participants in international affairs, it becomes especially important that our educational system produce individuals who have the facility to communicate with these peoples, not on our terms but in their own tongues. The lack of emphasis on foreign language training in the United States is demonstrated by the fact that although the Chinese language is spoken by more than twice as many persons in the world as English, as recently as six years ago only about five secondary schools in this country taught Chinese.[1] According to a recent survey conducted by the U.S. Office of Education, only 24 per cent of the students enrolled in public high schools in 1962 were taking a modern foreign language, and only one-half of one per cent of high school students were enrolled in a foreign language beyond the third year.[2] All of this underscores the necessity for a wider choice of foreign language courses at all levels of the educational system, more competent language teachers, an earlier beginning to language instruction, and most important, a greater encouragement of students to prepare themselves to speak or read one or more languages in addition to English.

One of the points on which critics of the so-called progressive movement in American education have frequently focused their sharpest attacks has been the degree to which courses in American government, history, civics, and the like should emphasize or indicate the faults in our system and the mistakes we have made as a nation or as individual representatives of our country during the past. The critics argue that we have been spending too much time derogating our national heroes and pointing out difficulties with the way we run our country and not enough time emphasizing the things of which we ought to be proud in our heritage as well as in our current political system. Many have also objected to discussions of the relative advantages and disadvantages of competing political systems, including communism, in elementary and secondary school class-rooms.

One of the things that is vitally needed throughout American society today is a greater appreciation on the part of its citizens of the very great strengths of our political system and, indeed, of our society itself. It is perhaps symptomatic of the impact of rapid change on the huge and intransigent bureaucratic structures that character-ize our society that there is a tendency to become overwhelmed by the problems that beset us from every quarter and by a feeling of frustration at our inability to mobilize our resources to wipe them out with a single bold stroke. Change creates the desire for more change, and the more resources we have at our disposal the greater impatience we feel with the problems of implementing desirable reforms. One of the major characteristics of a democratic system is that it is not always possible to move as rapidly as one wishes—only a dictatorship makes possible rapid accommodations. Thus we must live with our frustrations, at least for a time. Hiding our difficulties from school children does little to make them disappear in the long run and may result in a far greater sense of failure and disillusionment when they must finally be confronted. An awareness of our systems' weaknesses is in no way antithetical to a wholehearted belief in its overall progress and advantages, as well as confidence in its ultimate triumph. In an age of shades of gray instead of blacks and whites we are beginning to realize that blind faith in something is often more of a hindrance than a help when it comes to articulating a point of view or convincing an opponent. On the other hand, an appreciation of the realistic strong points and weaknesses of the opposing point of view can add to the courage and forcefulness with which one is able to express his convictions.

Most important, the overall record can stand by itself without any help from those who would protect children's minds from the truth. The fact of the matter is that our system has worked longer and better than any other thus far devised. The evidence needs only to be presented completely, impartially, and sympathetically. It is almost a traditional characteristic of adults, whether they be parents, schoolteachers, or merely bystanders, that they underestimate the capabilities of children. Perhaps this has something to do with their insecurities and a need to perceive themselves as more sophisticated or enlightened or objective than their children. Whatever the cause, the effect is all too frequently an unnecessary and sometimes dan-gerous diffusion of the facts in the name of simplification in order to make them understandable to the younger generation. Thus we have the unwarranted glorification of heroes, the distortion of facts about our political leaders, the overemphasis of the "perfection" of our political system and the evils of our competitors', and in general the deletion of any degree of sophistication from the intellectual life of our children.

The development of intellectual sophistication takes time. It may be too much to expect a fifth-grader (or at least *most* fifth-graders) to achieve a clear understanding of the various factors that, for example, have gone into United States policy regarding Cuba. But it is the contention of this writer that (1) we are underestimating our children's capacities in this regard by a wide margin, and that (2) the changing nature of the world and the resulting demands that will be made on members of free societies like our own require drastic alterations in our approaches to such subjects as history, social studies, and government in our schools. Our capacity as a nation to deal with internal frustrations and to withstand pressures from without rests upon a combination of confidence, optimism, determination, and sophistication on the part of citizens. This can only be provided by an educational system that, while avoiding intellectual cynicism, is meticulous in its reverence for the truth.

There is considerable doubt as to whether our schools, as presently organized and operated, can meet these challenges. As we have pointed out, responsibility for education in this country has traditionally been left to the local community and to the state. It is exceptionally difficult for a provincially organized and locally controlled system to achieve a high degree of sensitivity to extra-community or, especially, extra-national affairs. The extent to which a school system does achieve such an awareness is likely to be closely related to the involvement of the community's citizens in national and international affairs. Where most of the people in the community are primarily oriented toward local problems, the outlook of the school is likely to be correspondingly narrow. As long as schools resist the various attempts to apply national standards or to establish minimum curriculum requirements on a nationwide basis, this situation probably will not be altered significantly—that is, unless local school board members become aware of the needs and exert a broadening influence, at best an uncertain occurrence.

Teachers provide an additional means by which a broader perspective may be introduced, but school boards tend to hire personnel who fit into the existing pattern, often locally raised and locally trained individuals. Thus the preoccupation of American schools with local problems, customs, and traditions would appear to be a self-perpetuating tendency; one that may require external remedies—for example the establishment of a national testing program—if we are to take any major steps forward in preparing children to handle the responsibilities of our increasingly complex and swift-moving world.

Provincialism of school systems is not the only problem that must be overcome before we can expect significant advances in the general level of sophistication of the population vis-à-vis international and national affairs. Thus far we have not been able to attract a sufficient number of even mediocre teachers into the field of education to meet the ever growing demand. If we were to add to the requirements for prospective elementary teachers that they should have strong preparation in history, languages, and the social sciences, as well as a high degree of intellectual sophistication and an awareness of the implications of foreign policy for everyday affairs, we would rule out all but a tiny minority of those who are teaching today. As has been pointed out above, we are not paying teachers enough, either in status or financial terms, to attract into the field the kinds of individuals that are needed. Nor for the most part have we been providing potential teachers with the kinds of substantive training in our teachers' colleges and schools of education that they need in order to create the proper climate of intellectual stimulation in their classrooms. Thus a reduction in the current emphasis on methods and greater stress on content, as is advocated by James Conant in *The Education of American Teachers,* would appear to be indicated. Another solution is to make better use of the few highly sophisticated and well-trained teachers we do have by letting them operate as master teachers with responsibility for helping several less well-trained teachers to work through some of these problems.

It is clear that some major changes are indicated in our general approach to education and the specific organization of our schools. Perhaps most important is the need for a renewed commitment to education, a willingness as a nation and as individual citizens to allocate a significantly greater share of our resources to the improvement of our schools, not so much in terms of physical facilities or allied services but for the purposes most central to the outcome of the educational process. Teachers' salaries must be raised not only above the subsistence level but enough to make it possible for schools to compete with business firms and other users of society's talent for the best manpower—and on a career basis. In addition to increased financial rewards for teachers, the professional characteristics of teaching as an occupation must be ensured and strengthened through an upgrading of the social status of teachers (which will come in part with higher salaries) and a decrease in the current bureaucratization of school systems wherever it leads to an encroachment on the freedom and independence of teachers. Increased resources also must be channeled into our teacher-training institutions, currently the weakest link in the entire system, if any significant progress is to be made in any of the areas mentioned above.

All of these remedies and recommendations have been made in the past and will no doubt be made again before they receive the required broad and active support of legislators, civil servants, and, most important, the general public. The tendency towards inaction is an inherent characteristic of our political system, especially where no great emergency is perceived (in the case of education by the time an emergency is declared it will be too late). But some steps in the right direction can be taken now, without massive redistribution of funds or administrative reorganization. We have indicated a few of the possible approaches.

The major point of this book has been the need for and the feasibility of a focus on the responsibility of the school to prepare children to solve the new problems that a rapidly changing society and world creates for its citizens. We can no longer be satisfied with schools that do not teach children (and not only the children of the upper classes but *all* new members of the society) to think for themselves and to re-evaluate new situations as they arise. A changing world and the unique and growing interdependence of the peoples in it has made the old techniques less relevant, if not obsolete. This is a place to start now: in the training of teachers, in the development of curriculum requirements, and above all, in the classroom. It will not be easy since more than anything else it depends on the willingness of adults to admit the vulnerability of their ideas and techniques in a changing world. But the time is short, perhaps much shorter than we realize. And the very future of our civilization is at stake. Let us look forward to the day when we can be glad that our future is in the hands of our school children.

FOOTNOTES

INTRODUCTION

1. Robert L. Ebel, "The Social Consequences of Educational Testing." Paper presented at the 1963 Invitational Conference on Testing Problems, sponsored by the Educational Testing Service, Hotel Roosevelt, New York, November 2, 1963.

CHAPTER ONE

1. See Wilbert E. Moore, *Social Change* (Englewood Cliffs, N.J.: Prentice-Hall, Inc., 1963), pp. 6–11, for a brief discussion of this problem. Moore uses the term "function" to refer to "the intended or unintended consequences of action" (p. 28).

2. Vincent Ostrom, "Education and Politics," in *Social Forces Influencing American Education,* ed. Nelson B. Henry (Chicago: The National Society for the Study of Education, 1961), pp. 10–12. Distributed by the University of Chicago Press.

3. Burton R. Clark, *Educating the Expert Society* (San Francisco: Chandler Publishing Company, 1962), p. 11.

4. *Ibid.,* p. 12.

5. *Ibid.,* p. 15.

6. *Ibid.,* p. 15.

7. B. F. Skinner, *Walden Two* (New York: Macmillan Company, 1962).

8. Ralph Linton, *The Study of Man* (New York: D. Appleton-Century Co., 1936).

9. Although most people think immediately of racial discrimination in this context, it should be noted that race is only one of several ascribed characteristics that influence the allocation of positions. Sex is a more important basis for discrimination in many situations, for example.

10. Alexander W. Astin, " 'Productivity' of Undergraduate Institutions," *Science,* CXXXVI (April 13, 1962).

11. Peter H. and Alice S. Rossi, "Some Effects of Parochial School Education in America," *Daedalus* (Spring, 1961).

12. *Ibid.,* p. 324.

13. *Ibid.,* p. 323.

14. *Ibid.,* p. 324.

CHAPTER TWO

1. For an extensive discussion of the use of the terms *position, status,* and *role,* see Neal C. Gross, Ward S. Mason, and Alexander W. MacEachern, *Explorations in Role Analysis: Studies of the School Superintendency Role* (New York: John Wiley and Sons, 1958); and Harry M. Johnson, *Sociology: A Systematic Introduction* (New York: Harcourt, Brace and Company, 1960), pp. 15–39.

2. For example, see John W. Riley, Jr. and Matilda White Riley, "Sociological Perspectives on the Use of New Educational Media," in *New Teaching Aids for the American Classroom,* U.S. Department of Health, Education, and Welfare (Washington, D.C.: Office of Education, 1960).

3. *Ibid.,* p. 32.

4. Richard Schmuck, "Some Relationships of Peer Liking Patterns in the Classroom to Pupil Attitudes and Achievement," *The School Review*, LXXI, No. 3 (Autumn 1963), 337–359.

5. James S. Coleman, *The Adolescent Society* (New York: The Free Press of Glencoe, 1961).

6. Riley and Riley, *op. cit.*, pp. 34–35.

7. D. C. McClelland, J. W. Atkinson, R. A. Clark, and E. L. Lowell, *The Achievement Motive* (New York: Appleton-Century-Crofts, 1953); and *Studies in Motivation*, ed. D. C. McClelland (New York: Appleton-Century-Crofts, 1955).

8. Talcott Parsons, "The School Class as a Social System: Some of Its Functions in American Society." Unpublished paper. Quoted in Riley and Riley, *op. cit.*, p. 37.

9. See Neal Gross *et al.*, *op. cit.*

10. Robin Williams, *American Society, A Sociological Interpretation*, 2nd ed. (New York: Knopf, 1960), p. 309.

11. U.S. Department of Health, Education, and Welfare, Office of Education, *Statistics of State School Systems, 1959–60* (Washington, D.C.: U.S. Government Printing Office, 1963), p. 13.

12. For a summary of certification requirements in the various states, see Earl W. Armstrong and T. M. Stinnett, *A Manual on Certification Requirements for School Personnel in the United States*, 1961 ed. (National Commission on Teacher Education and Professional Standards, National Education Association), p. 33.

CHAPTER THREE

1. Burton R. Clark, *Educating the Expert Society* (San Francisco: Chandler Publishing Company, 1962), p. 63.

2. Wilbert E. Moore, *Social Change* (Englewood Cliffs, N.J.: Prentice-Hall Inc., 1963), p. 2.

3. Wilbert E. Moore, "Predicting Discontinuities in Social Change," *American Sociological Review*, XXIX, No. 3 (June 1964), 331–338.

4. U.S. Department of Health, Education, and Welfare, Office of Education, *Enrollment, Teachers, and Schoolhousing*, Final Report, Fall 1963 (Washington, D.C.: U.S. Government Printing Office, 1964).

5. Eleanor H. Bernert and Charles B. Nam, "Demographic Factors Affecting American Education," in *Social Forces Influencing American Education*, ed. Nelson B. Henry (Chicago: The National Society for the Study of Education, 1961), pp. 89–119. Distributed by the University of Chicago Press. P. 89.

6. *Ibid.*, p. 91.

7. U.S. Department of Health, Education, and Welfare, *Biennial Survey of Education, 1955–56*, Section II, *Statistics of Local School Systems: "Suburban Cities,"* chap. 3 (Washington, D.C.: Government Printing Office, 1960). Cited in Bernert and Nam, *op. cit.*, p. 102.

8. Bernert and Nam, *op. cit.*, p. 93.

9. *Ibid.*, p. 107.

10. *Ibid.,* p. 108.

11. Source: U.S. Census Bureau, 1960 Census. Reported in *The World Almanac* (New York: New York World Telegram Corp., 1964).

CHAPTER FOUR

1. George Herbert Mead, *Mind, Self, and Society* (Chicago: University of Chicago Press, 1934).

2. See Max Rafferty, *What They Are Doing to Your Children* (New York: New American Library, 1963).

3. Omar K. Moore and Alan R. Anderson, "Autotelic Folk Models," *Sociological Quarterly* I (Summer 1960), 203–216.

4. *Ibid.*

5. James S. Coleman, *The Adolescent Society* (New York: The Free Press of Glencoe, 1961).

6. *Ibid.,* p. 5.

7. Vincent Ostrom, "Education and Politics," in *Social Forces Influencing American Education,* ed. Nelson B. Henry (Chicago: The National Society for the Study of Education, 1961), p. 20. Distributed by the University of Chicago Press. Jefferson quote from a Letter to Colonel Yancy, 1816, in *Thomas Jefferson on Democracy,* ed. Saul K. Padover (New York: Penguin Books, Inc., 1939), p. 89.

8. Fred M. Newmann, "Consent of the Governed," *The School Review,* LXXI, No. 4 (Winter 1963), 421.

9. C. Roy E. Horton, "American Freedom and the Values of Youth." Unpublished Doctoral Dissertation. (Purdue University, 1955.)

10. James S. Coleman, "Research Program in the effects of Games with Simulated Environments in Secondary Education," Report No. 1, October 1963 (Johns Hopkins University, Department of Social Relations).

CHAPTER FIVE

1. Max Rafferty, *What They Are Doing to Your Children* (New York: New American Library, 1963), p. 77.

2. Max Rafferty, in his recent attack on "progressive education," reserves his sharpest barbs for such courses as "social living," "student leadership," "senior problems," and "life adjustment." Although one can hardly find fault with his contention that such courses are no substitute for rigorous instruction in the basic subjects, one wonders to what extent American elementary and secondary schools *actually* offer such courses in place of (or even in addition to) more traditional subjects. On the basis of findings of a nationwide survey of courses and enrollments by the U.S. Office of Education in 1960–1961 (Grace S. Wright, "Summary of Offerings and Enrollments in High School Subjects," Office of Education Bulletin No. OE-24010, June 1964), it seems probable that Rafferty's position, while sincere, is overstated.

3. Omar Khayyam Moore, "Autotelic Responsive Environments and Exceptional Children" (Hamden, Conn.: Responsive Environments Foundation, Inc., 1963), p. 5.

4. *Ibid.*

5. Merle L. Borrowman, "Traditional Values and the Shaping of

American Education," in *Social Forces Influencing American Education,* ed. Henry B. Nelson (Chicago: The National Society for the Study of Education, 1961), p. 161. Distributed by the University of Chicago Press.

6. Lest I be accused of ignoring the innovative side of the teaching function, it should be made clear that good teachers do contribute to knowledge in the process of developing material for courses, writing lectures, in daily interaction with students, and the like.

7. See Burton R. Clark, *The Open Door College* (New York: McGraw-Hill Book Company, Inc., 1960).

8. Wilbur Schramm, "Mass Media and Educational Policy," *Social Forces Influencing American Education, op. cit.,* pp. 210-211.

CHAPTER SIX

1. David A. Goslin, Roberta E. Raynor, and Barbara A. Hallock, *The Use of Standardized Tests in Elementary Schools,* Technical Report No. 2 on The Social Consequences of Testing (New York: Russell Sage Foundation, 1965).

2. John T. Dailey, "A Survey of the Use of Tests in Public High Schools." Paper presented at the Twelfth Annual Conference of Directors of State Testing Programs at Princeton, N.J., February 1962. Mimeographed.

3. J. C. Daniels, "The Effects of Streaming in the Primary School," *British Journal of Educational Psychology,* DXXI (1961), 119-127.

4. David A. Goslin, *The Search for*

Ability (New York: Russell Sage Foundation, 1963), pp. 177-178.

5. Dael L. Wolfle, "Diversity of Talent," *American Psychologist,* XV (August 1960), 539.

6. See Leon J. Yarrow, "Separation from Parents During Early Childhood," in *Review of Child Development Research,* Vol. 1, ed. Martin L. and Lois Hoffman (New York: Russell Sage Foundation, 1964).

7. William H. Sewell, "The Educational and Occupational Perspectives of Rural Youth." Paper prepared for the National Conference on Problems of Rural Youth in a Changing Environment, September 1963.

8. Martin Deutsch, "Minority Group and Class Status as Related to Social and Personality Factors in Scholastic Achievement," *Society of Applied Anthropology Monograph,* 1960, No. 2.

9. Burton R. Clark, *Educating the Expert Society* (San Francisco: Chandler Publishing Co., 1962), p. 96.

10. David Gottlieb, "Teaching and Students: The Views of Negro and White Teachers," *Sociology of Education,* XXXVII, No. 4 (Summer 1964), 345-353.

11. The alternative, of course, is the elimination of slums. Some educators would argue that as long as it is true that schools require a particular kind of community environment in order to function effectively (e.g., sympathetic and interested parents, financial and personnel resources, et cetera) no real progress will be made until we have elimi-

nated social environments that are hostile to the educational process.

CHAPTER SEVEN

1. Charles E. Bidwell, "The School as a Formal Organization," chap. 25, in *Handbook of Administration and Organization Theory*, ed. James G. March (Chicago: Rand McNally and Company, in press).

2. Board of Education of the City of New York, *New York Public Schools: Facts and Figures*, 1963–64, pp. 52–53.

3. Charles Bidwell, *op. cit.*

4. *Ibid.*

5. *Ibid.*

6. *Ibid.*

7. Myron Liberman, "The Influence of Teachers' Organizations upon American Education," in *Social Forces Influencing American Education*, ed. Nelson B. Henry (Chicago: The National Society for the Study of Education, 1961), pp. 182–202. Distributed by the University of Chicago Press.

8. Bidwell, *op, cit.*

9. Talcott Parsons, "The Classroom as a Social System: Some of its Functions in American Society," *Harvard Educational Review*, XXIX (Fall 1959), 297–318.

10. U.S. Department of Health, Education, and Welfare, Office of Education, *Enrollment, Teachers, and Schoolhousing*, Final Report, Fall 1963 (Washington, D.C.: U.S. Government Printing Office, 1964).

11. Ward S. Mason, Robert J. Dressel, and Robert K. Bain, "Sex Role and the Career Orientations of Beginning Teachers," *Harvard Educational Review*, XXIX, No. 4 (Fall 1959); and Ward S. Mason, *The Beginning Teacher: Status and Career Orientations* (Washington, D.C.: U.S. Department of Health, Education, and Welfare, Office of Education, U.S. Government Printing Office, 1961).

12. Theodore Bienenstock and William Sayres, *Problems in Job Satisfaction Among Junior High School Teachers* (Albany, N.Y.: University of the State of New York, Division of Research, June 1963), p. 28.

CHAPTER EIGHT

1. Carnegie Corporation, *Annual Report*, 1963, p. 22. The Report indicates that this number has grown to more than seventy-five schools, in part due to Carnegie support.

2. Survey conducted by the Modern Language Association under contract with the U.S. Office of Education. Reported in *Higher Education*, XX, No. 8 (May 1964).

BIBLIOGRAPHY

INTRODUCTION

There are relatively few general works in the field of educational sociology. Among the best of these is Orville G. Brim, Jr.'s, concise summary of existing and needed research in the field which was prepared for the American Sociological Association. A more detailed but perhaps less coherent view of many of the problems in this area may be gained from the compilation of articles by Halsey, Floud, and Anderson and the *NSSE Yearbook*, edited by Nelson Henry.

Of the many introductory textbooks in sociology, Harry Johnson's has the distinction of being both sophisticated and relatively theoretical in orientation. George Homan's *The Human Group* is a model of the insightful merging of theory and empirical observation in the social sciences.

Brim, Orville G., Jr. *Sociology and the Field of Education*. New York, Russell Sage Foundation, 1958.

Brookover, Wilbur. *A Sociology of Education*. New York, The American Book Company, 1955.

Durkheim, Emile. *Education et Sociologie*. Paris, F. Alcan, 1922.

Ehlers, Henry, and G. C. Lee, eds. *Crucial Issues in Education*. New York, Henry Holt and Company, 1959.

Gross, Neal. "Some Contributions of Sociology to the Field of Education," *Harvard Educational Review*, XXIX (1959), 275–287.

Halsey, A. G., Jean Floud, and C. Arnold Anderson, eds. *Education, Economy, and Society*. Glencoe, Ill., The Free Press of Glencoe, 1961.

Henry, Nelson B., ed. *Social Forces Influencing American Education*. Chicago, The National Society for the Study of Education, 1961. Distributed by the University of Chicago Press.

Homans, G. C. *The Human Group*. New York, Harcourt, Brace and World, Inc., 1950.

Johnson, Harry M. *Sociology: A Systematic Introduction*. New York, Harcourt, Brace and World, Inc., 1960.

Merton, R. K., L. Broom, and L. S. Cottrell, Jr., eds. *Sociology Today: Problems and Prospects*. New York, Basic Books, Inc., 1959.

Page, Charles H., ed. *Sociology and Contemporary Education*, New York, Random House, 1963.

Raywid, Mary Anne. *The Ax-Grinders*. New York, The Macmillan Co., 1962.

Waller, W. *The Sociology of Teaching*. New York, John Wiley and Sons, Inc., 1932.

CHAPTER ONE

Very similar to the present volume, although somewhat narrower in its aim, is Burton Clark's *Educating the Expert Society*. This highly readable book contains much useful data on the problems of preparing students to live in an age of advanced technology. A broader view not only of education but of the various other institutions in society is provided by Robin Williams in *American Society*.

For the theoretically oriented student of sociology, the volumes edited by Merton, and Parsons and Shils are of considerable relevance.

Chandler, B. J., Lindley J. Stiles, and John I. Kitsuse, eds. *Education in Urban Society*. New York, Dodd, Mead and Company, 1962.

Clark, Burton R. *Educating the Expert Society*. San Francisco, Chandler Publishing Company, 1962.

Counts, George S. *Education and the Foundations of Human Freedom.* Pittsburgh, University of Pittsburgh, 1963.

Dewey, John. *The Public and Its Problems.* New York, Henry Holt and Co., 1927.

Halsey, A. G., Jean Floud, and C. Arnold Anderson, eds. *Education, Economy, and Society.* Glencoe, Ill., The Free Press of Glencoe, 1961.

Havighurst, R. J., and B. L. Neugarten. *Society and Education.* Boston, Allyn and Bacon, 1962.

Katz, Irwin. "Review of Evidence Relating to Effects of Desegregation on the Intellectual Performance of Negroes." ONR Technical Report No. 8, February 1964. Mimeographed paper.

Merton, R. K., ed. *Social Theory and Social Structure: Toward the Codification of Theory and Research.* Glencoe, Ill., Free Press of Glencoe, 1957.

Parsons, Talcott, and Edward A. Shils, eds. *Foundations of Modern Sociological Theory.* Glencoe, Ill., The Free Press of Glencoe, 1961.

Sumner, W. G. *Folkways: A Study of the Sociological Importance of Usages, Manners, Customs, Mores, and Morals.* New York, Ginn, 1906.

Whitehead, A. N. *The Aims of Education and Other Essays.* New York, Macmillan Co., 1929.

Williams, R. M., Jr. *American Society: A Sociological Interpretation,* Rev. ed. New York, Alfred A. Knopf, 1961.

CHAPTER TWO

One of the best existing studies of role conflict and of the characteristics of administrative roles in school systems is Neal Gross's *Explorations in Role Analysis.* This work is also notable for an exposition of the various concepts and related terms that make up role theory. August Hollingshead, James Coleman, and Howard Becker have all contributed useful insights into the nature of student society and its relation to the school.

Becker, Howard S. "Social Class and Teacher-Pupil Relationships," in Blain E. Mercer and Edwin R. Carr, eds. *Education and the Social Order.* New York, Rinehart and Co., Inc., 1957.

Bloomberg, W., Jr., and M. Sunshine. *Suburban Power Structures and Public Education.* Syracuse N.Y., Syracuse University Press, 1963.

Carter, Richard F., and John Sutthof. *Communities and Their Schools.* Institute for Communication Research, School of Education, Stanford Calif., Stanford University, 1960.

Charters, W. W., Jr. "Social Class Analysis and the Control of Public Education," *Harvard Educational Review,* XXIII (1953), 268–283.

Coleman, James S. *The Adolescent Society.* Glencoe, Ill., The Free Press of Glencoe, 1961.

Conant, James B. *The American High School Today.* New York, McGraw-Hill Book Co., 1959.

Gordon, C. W. *The Social System of the High School.* Glencoe, Ill., The Free Press of Glencoe, 1957.

Gross, Neal, *et al. Explorations in Role Analysis: Studies of the School Superintendency Role.* New York, John Wiley and Sons, 1958.

Gross, Neal. *Who Runs Our Schools?* New York, John Wiley and Sons, Inc., 1958.

Hollingshead, August B. *Elmtown's Youth.* New York, John Wiley and Sons, 1949.

Homans, George C. *Social Behavior:*

Its Elementary Forms. New York, Harcourt, Brace and World, 1961.

Merton, R. K. *Social Theory and Social Structure.* Glencoe, Ill., The Free Press of Glencoe, 1957.

Parsons, Talcott. *The Social System.* Glencoe, Ill., The Free Press of Glencoe, 1951.

Stiles, Lindley J., ed. *The Teacher's Role in American Society.* New York, Harper and Bros., 1957.

Waller, W. *Sociology of Teaching.* New York, John Wiley and Sons, 1932.

CHAPTER THREE

The books and articles that have treated one or another aspect of social change are far too numerous to even list here; consequently, only a representative sprinkling follows. Among those who have concerned themselves with the topic of change in its broadest context, William F. Ogburn, Pitirim Sorokin, and Wilbert Moore have made significant contributions. Ogburn's *The Social Effects of Aviation* is a classic example of the sociological analysis of the impact of a technological innovation on society.

Bogue, Donald J. *The Population of the United States.* Glencoe, Ill., The Free Press of Glencoe, 1959.

Conant, James B. *Slums and Suburbs: A Commentary on Schools in Metropolitan Areas.* New York, McGraw-Hill Book Company, Inc, 1961.

Fusco, Gene C. "Preparing the City Child for His School," *School Life,* XLVI, No. 6 (May 1964).

Gottmann, Jean. *Megalopolis: Urbanized North-eastern Seaboard of the United States.* New York, Twentieth Century Fund, 1961.

Hatt, P. K., and A. J. Reiss, Jr., eds. *Cities in Society: Revised*

Reader in Urban Sociology. Glencoe, Ill., The Free Press of Glencoe, 1957.

Hauser, Philip M., and Otis Dudley Duncan. *The Study of Population.* Chicago, University of Chicago Press, 1959.

Henry, Nelson B., ed. *Social Forces Influencing American Education.* Chicago, The National Society for the Study of Education, 1961. Distributed by the University of Chicago Press.

Moore, Wilbert E. "Predicting Discontinuities in Social Change," *American Sociological Review,* XXIX, No. 3 (June 1964), 331–338.

Moore, Wilbert E. *Social Change.* Englewood Cliffs, N.J., Prentice Hall, 1963.

Ogburn, William F. *Social Change.* New York, Viking Press, 1938. Originally published by Huebsch, 1922.

Ogburn, William F. *The Social Effects of Aviation.* Boston, Houghton Mifflin, 1946.

Sorokin, Pitirim A. *Social and Cultural Dynamics.* 4 vols. New York, American Book Company, 1937–1941.

Taeuber, Conrad, and Irene B. Taeuber. *The Changing Population of the United States.* New York, John Wiley and Sons, Inc., 1958.

CHAPTER FOUR

Brim, O. G., Jr. "Socialization Through the Life Cycle," *Items.* XVIII, No. 1 (March 1964), Social Science Research Council.

Borrowman, Merle L. "Traditional Values and the Shaping of American Education," in *Social Forces Influencing American Education,* ed. Nelson B. Henry. Chicago, The National Society for the Study of Education, 1961. Distributed by the University of Chicago Press.

Coleman, James S. *The Adolescent*

Society. Glencoe, Ill., The Free Press of Glencoe, 1961.

Conant, James B. *Education and Liberty: The Role of the Schools in a Modern Democracy*. Cambridge, Mass., Harvard University Press, 1953.

Diamond, Stanley E. "Citizenship Education," in *Encyclopedia of Educational Research*, 3rd ed., New York, 1960, pp. 206–210.

Edelman, Murray. "Symbols and Political Quiescence," *American Political Science Review*, LIV (1960), 695–704.

Mead, G. H. *Mind, Self and Society from the Standpoint of a Social Behaviorist*. Chicago, University of Chicago Press, 1934.

Ostrom, Vincent. "Education and Politics," in *Social Forces Influencing American Education*, ed. Nelson B. Henry. Chicago, The National Society for the Study of Education, 1961. Distributed by The University of Chicago Press.

Patterson, Franklin. *High Schools for a Free Society: Education for Citizenship in American Secondary Schools*. Glencoe, Ill., The Free Press of Glencoe, 1960.

CHAPTER FIVE

The development and encouragement of creativity on the part of students has been a topic of increasing concern to educators, psychologists and others during the past decade. Gruber, *et al*, Moore, and Torrance have provided provocative discussions of this critical topic, and some of the difficulties in identifying the potentially creative child are enumerated in *The Search for Ability* (see Chapter 6). Mathew Miles's collection of articles on the problems of educational innovation is a must for the student interested in this topic.

Coleman, James S. "Playing Politics in the Classroom," *The Johns Hopkins Magazine* (October 1963), 14–20.

Dewey, John. *Logic: The Theory of Inquiry*. New York, Henry Holt and Co., 1938.

Evans, L. H., and G. E. Arnstein, eds. *Automation and the Challenge to Education*. Washington, D.C., National Education Association, 1962.

Gruber, Howard E., Glenn Terrell, and Michael Wertheimer, eds. *Contemporary Approaches to Creative Thinking*. New York, Atherton Press, 1962.

Maccoby, Eleanor E. "Effects of the Mass Media," in Hoffman, Martin L., and Lois W. Hoffman, *Review of Child Development Research*. New York, Russell Sage Foundation, 1964.

Medsker, Leland L. *The Junior College: Progress and Prospect*. New York, McGraw-Hill Book Company, Inc., 1960.

Miles, Mathew B., ed. *Innovation in Education*. New York, Bureau of Publications, Teachers College, Columbia University, 1964.

Moore, Omar K. "Autotelic Responsive Environments and Exceptional Children," Hamden, Conn., Responsive Environments Foundation, Inc., 1963.

Moore, Omar K., and Alan R. Anderson. "Autotelic Folk-Models," *The Sociological Quarterly*, I (1960).

Moore, Omar K., and Alan R. Anderson. "Some Puzzling Aspects of Social Interaction," *The Review of Metaphysics*, XV, No. 3 (March 1962).

Moore, Omar K., and Alan R. Anderson. "The Structure of Personality," *The Review of Metaphysics*. XVI, No. 2 (December 1962).

Rafferty, Max. *What They Are Doing*

to Your Children. New York, The New American Library, 1963.

Rickover, H. G. *Education and Freedom.* New York, E. P. Dutton and Company, Inc., 1960.

Schramm, W., J. Lyle, and I. de S. Pool. *The People Look at Educational Television.* Stanford, Calif., Stanford University Press, 1963.

Educational Television: The Next Ten Years, Institute for Communication Research, Stanford University, 1962.

Torrance, E. P. *Education and the Creative Potential.* Minneapolis, University of Minnesota Press, 1963.

CHAPTER SIX

General works on social stratification and social mobility in America include those by Kahl, Bendix, and Lipset, and Lipset and Bendix. The relation between education and social status is examined in the books by Halsey and Warner *et al.,* and the articles by Havighurst and Sewell *et al.* An especially provocative and entertaining treatment of the possible effects of a stratification system based entirely on merit is provided by Michael Young in *The Rise of the Meritocracy.*

Anti-Defamation League of B'nai B'rith. *The Treatment of Minorities in Secondary School Textbooks.* New York, 1961.

Bendix, R., and S. M. Lipset, eds. *Class, Status and Power: A Reader in Social Stratification.* Glencoe, Ill., The Free Press of Glencoe, 1953.

Clark, Burton R. *The Open Door College: A Case Study.* New York, McGraw-Hill Book Company, 1960.

Dexter, Lewis A. *The Tyranny of*

Schooling. New York, Basic Books, Inc., 1964.

Ellis, Robert A., and W. Clayton Lane. "Structural Supports for Upward Mobility," *American Sociological Review,* XXVIII, No. 5 (October 1963), 743–756.

Goslin, David A. *The Search for Ability.* New York, Russell Sage Foundation, 1963.

Halsey, A. H., ed. *Ability and Educational Opportunity.* Organization for Economic Co-operation and Development, 1961.

Havighurst, Robert J. "Social-Class Influences on American Education," in *Social Forces Influencing American Education,* ed. Nelson B. Henry. Chicago, National Society for the Study of Education, 1961. Distributed by the University of Chicago Press.

Kahl, J. A. *The American Class Structure.* New York, Holt, Rinehart and Winston, 1957.

Lipset, S. M., and R. Bendix. *Social Mobility in Industrial Society.* Berkeley and Los Angeles, University of California Press, 1959.

Sanford, Nevitt, ed. *The American College.* New York, John Wiley and Sons, 1962.

Sewell, W. H., A. O. Haller, and M. A. Straus. "Social Status and Educational and Occupational Aspiration," *American Sociological Review,* XXII (1957), 67–73.

Torrance, E. P., ed. *Talent and Education.* Minneapolis, The University of Minnesota Press, 1960.

Warner, W. Lloyd, Robert J. Havighurst, and Martin B. Loeb. *Who Shall be Educated?* New York, Harper and Bros., 1960.

Wolfle, Dael L. *America's Resources of Specialized Talent.* New York, Harper and Bros., 1954.

Young, Donald. "In Praise of Specialization," in *Both Human and Humane,* eds. Charles E. Boew and Roy F. Nichols. Philadelphia, University of Pennsylvania Press, pp. 213–224.

Young, Michael. *The Rise of the Meritocracy.* London, Thames and Hudson, 1958.

CHAPTER SEVEN

The literature on organizations is extensive and varied in its focus. Major theoretical books in the field include those by Herbert Simon, Peter Blau and Amitai Etzioni. Much of the research that has been done in this area is summarized in the *Handbook of Administration and Organization Theory,* edited by James March. William H. Whyte's *The Organization Man* remains a classic commentary on modern industrial society.

Blau, P. M. *The Dynamics of Bureaucracy.* 2nd ed. Chicago, University of Chicago Press, 1963.

Blau, P. M., and W. R. Scott. *Formal Organizations.* San Francisco, Chandler Publishing Co., 1962.

Boulding, Kenneth. *The Organizational Revolution.* New York, Harper and Bros., 1953.

Callahan, Raymond E. *Education and the Cult of Efficiency.* Chicago, The University of Chicago Press, 1962.

Caplow, Theodore, and Reece J. McGee. *The Academic Marketplace.* Indianapolis, Basic Books, Inc., 1958.

Cicourel, Aaron V., and John I. Kitsuse. *The Educational Decision-Makers.* New York, The Bobbs-Merrill Company, Inc., 1963.

Coleman, James S. *The Adolescent Society.* Glencoe, Ill., The Free Press of Glencoe, 1961.

Committee for Economic Development, Research and Policy Committee. *Paying for Better Public Schools,* New York, 1960.

Conant, James B. *The Education of American Teachers.* New York, McGraw-Hill Book Company, Inc., 1963.

Etzioni, Amitai. *Complex Organization.* New York, Holt, Rinehart and Winston, 1961.

Gross, Neal. *Who Runs Our Schools?* New York, John Wiley and Sons, Inc., 1958.

Harvard Educational Review, *Guidance: An Examination,* XXXII (Fall 1962).

Katz, Fred E. "The School as a Complex Social Organization," *Harvard Educational Review,* XXXIV, No. 3 (Summer 1964), 428–455.

Kellogg, W. K., Foundation. *Toward Improved School Administration,* Battle Creek, Mich., 1961.

Lieberman, Myron. *Education as a Profession.* Englewood Cliffs, N.J., Prentice Hall, 1956.

Lipham, James M., *et al. Administrative Organization in Education.* Chicago, Midwest Administration Center, University of Chicago, 1958.

March, James G. *Handbook of Administration and Organization Theory.* Chicago, Rand McNally, in press.

Simon, Herbert A. *Administrative Behavior,* 2nd ed. New York, The Macmillan Co., 1957.

Weber, Max. *Essays in Sociology,* trans. H. H. Gerth and C. Wright Mills. New York, Oxford University Press, 1946.

Whyte, W. H. *The Organization Man.* New York, Simon and Schuster, 1956.

INDEX

A